Praise for *Forty-Two*

"Forty-Two *is more than a book; it's a tried and true roadmap to finishing well. I know of no better person than Steve Alessi to be our guide!*"

Lee Domingue
Founder, Kingdom Builders
Founder & CEO, AppOne, Cyrus Partners, GrowLeader, & m360

"*My heart is so stirred by this powerful new book by my dear friend Pastor Steve Alessi. I know the man and I honor the message that he is called to release.* Forty-Two *is a powerful reminder that, no matter the obstacle you face, you are called to get back up, dust yourself off, and fight for your future and purpose. Steve takes you on a journey from the crossroads of tragedy and triumph. He shows us that God will reach into the depths of your situation and restore hope. This book declares that we must hold on, for God is still in charge!*"

Pat Schatzline
Evangelist, Author, and CEO
Remnant Ministries International

"As long as I have known Steve Alessi, I have witnessed him roll with life's punches and come back stronger each time. I won't spoil his story—you'll come back stronger too when you read it for yourself. What I can share is that God changed Steve's life in the span of forty-two minutes. And God will change your life when you let the words of this book sink in."

Rev. Samuel Rodriguez
Author, Film Producer, & Lead Pastor of New Season Church
President & CEO, NHCLC

"As Steve's sister, this was the first time I really understood his play-by-play journey after that dark day he calls the "forty-two minutes." It broke my heart to read about the fear and helplessness he experienced, especially for someone who normally feels in control of his own world. A recommended read if you're looking to understand how to move through the scariest moments of uncertainty."

Deborah Alessi Giarratana
Film Producer
Machine Gun Preacher & The Tiger Rising

"This book is a must read! I was drawn in from page one, reading Steve's story, and I already knew the ending. If you are looking for practical ways to push beyond your limits and live a courageous life, this book is for you."

Martha Munizzi
Gospel Recording Artist & Co-Lead Pastor
EpicLife Church, Orlando, FL

"This book is a brilliant guide to persevering and getting back up when life's got you down."

Marcus Mecum
Senior Pastor, 7 Hills Church

"I wish I'd had this book when my dad (my best friend) died unexpectedly at 56. I couldn't imagine how I was going to go on...much less, fill his big ministry shoes. If you've ever been gut-kicked and left face down in the dirt, my friend Steve Alessi knows how to get back up and keep fighting. It's funny, when we're flat on our backs God suddenly has no problem getting our undivided attention. This book teaches that some of life's greatest lessons are learned while we're in 'survival mode.' It's encouraging to know that it's never too late for us to make adjustments...and still finish well!"

David Crank
Author, Speaker, Senior Pastor of FaithChurch.com

Steve Alessi

Forty

Two

A Guide To Finishing Well When
You Were Almost Finished

Forty-Two

ISBN: 978-1-955362-12-2

Published by
STORY CHORUS

Learn more at StoryChorus.com

Dedication

To my Dad. Your example of strength throughout your eighty-four years taught me how to never surrender. Up to the day you passed, you would tell me how to do things. Oh, how I wish I could hear you speak today. Your words are what I hear in my ears as I carry on our Alessi name, as my story is actually our story.

To my Mom. Your example of how to fight for your family deserves to be celebrated and honored. You infused our home with the DNA of a fighter. I'd like to think I was a good student in your classroom even though I wasn't in school. We're enjoying some special days now as you continue to live your beautiful life. Dad would be proud of you; I know I sure am.

To my mother-in-law, Faith. When you had to make the tough call for your family, you didn't falter one bit. That inspired your daughter and me to keep up the good fight of faith. It also showed us that goodness in life is worth going to battle for. Due to that, your children's children's children are calling you blessed.

Contents

Foreword

I sat with a friend named Grace at a local coffee shop. We'd been talking for nearly an hour—and now shared tears started to fall. She had lost her husband to an all-too-common tragedy: a widowmaker heart attack. As a pastor, my heart is always ready to mourn with those who mourn and bring comfort. However, this time was different.

Statistically, her sorrow *should have been* mine. Over a decade ago, Steve, my husband, suffered the same type of heart attack, which he shares about in detail in this book. Only Steve lived, while Grace's husband died.

Her source of greatest pain was the place of my deepest gratitude.

Through the years I have met so many other wives whose husbands did not make it. Moms who lost children while mine were safely asleep at home. Why should we be so fortunate, when others have suffered so much?

It is a question that has weighed heavily on me in the years since Steve's incident. This feeling has a name: *survivor's guilt.* It's a devastating feeling of remorse that you survived the same kind of traumatic event someone else did not. It's as if your joy has come at the expense of someone else's. Even though that's untrue, it doesn't always feel like it.

I have come to realize that the only way to make sense of such a mixed blessing is to give glory to God and make the most of the days He has given us. In this way, survivor's guilt can become survivor's glory—not that we have done anything special and profound, but that God has done something special and profound *for us.*

Whether you've faced catastrophic health challenges, financial disaster, destroyed relationships, or anything in between, this is a book to help you move forward. To help you keep walking through flame and flood.

My husband shares his own journey of recovery, as well as the lessons he has learned about perseverance, rekindling a broken dreamer, and reigniting faith. He also provides practical advice for anyone going through a similar experience.

While this book is a practice in gratitude for a second chance, it is also a somber invitation to treat every breath as sacred. To greet each day with gratitude and purpose. In all my life, I've never met a person who can bring peace like my husband.

So this is our prayer: that you would experience the peace of God that surpasses all knowledge and understanding so you find the strength to finish well.

Mary Alessi

Introduction

In 708 B.C., the Olympics got its first overhaul.

Bare-knuckle boxing had been around since 3000 B.C., but it was several thousand years later when the ancient competitors began to wrap soft leather straps around their hands and forearms for their own protection.[1] Until then, it was raw pummeling, skin on skin.

Over time, those protective leather straps became harder, meaning that the boxer could still protect himself, but he could also do maximum damage to his opponent.[2] By the time the gladiators rolled around, boxing was thought to be too violent and was banned.[3]

---

[1] "Description of Boxing." *Olympics.com*, International Olympic Committee, 27 Apr. 2021, https://olympics.com/en/news/description-of-boxing.

[2] "History of the IOC." International Olympic Committee, January 17, 2022. https://olympics.com/ioc/ancient-olympic-games/the-sports-events.

[3] SportsGeeks, and Name *. "Top 10 Oldest Sports in the World." *SportsGeeks*, 23 Apr. 2022, https://sportsgeeks.net/oldest-sports-in-the-world/.

There were no weight classes, you see, and that meant that sometimes David had to fight Goliath. But it's just those bouts that always captivated me when I was young.

I've loved boxing since I was a boy. From watching Ali fight Frazier, Sugar Ray Leonard fight "Marvelous" Marvin Hagler, or Cuban fighter Teófilo Stevenson in the Olympics, I've often thought about the amount of training that goes into each fight—especially when an underdog squares off with a giant. A fighter is trained to go into the ring with both hands blazing. But I often wondered, after the punch they never saw coming which sent them to the mat, were they trained to get back up?

Unlike boxing, there are no weight classes in life. Featherweights will battle heavy weights. Things happen that we feel woefully unable to fight through; big events throw haymakers from out of nowhere. They knock the wind out of us and even break our hearts.

A healthy heartbeat has both peaks and valleys. If you're flatlining, you're not living. That's a lot like life, the pattern of peaks and valleys, though it's not pleasant to think about. We face big opponents, those moments that knock us to the ground and make us wonder who thought we could stand a chance in such an unfair fight. In the valley, we don't think there will ever be another peak.

I know this personally. I've lived it.

I was down for the count, wondering if life was over, heart-broken, unsure how to get up off the mat. But I did.

What I want to do is not only tell you how to get up off the mat so you can get to another peak in life, but also to show you the value of the valleys. They have the potential to not just

A healthy heartbeat has both peaks and valleys. If you're flatlining, you're not living.

be an unavoidable pattern to dread, but instead, to be the path to reawakening you to a new life, one full of incredible dreams you thought impossible.

Maybe you thought you weren't up for the fight, that the opponent is too big. I'm here to show you otherwise.

Chapter
One

The Punch You Don't See Coming

I didn't know it, but my life was about to change. In thirty-six hours, I would brush that rice-paper-thin veil between life and death, surviving by a sliver of a sliver. It would be a tectonic shift, altering the course of both our family and our ministry forever. But for the moment, all I could focus on was the happy chatter of my family honoring me with a Father's Day lunch after a powerful service at Metro Life Church in our always-on city, Miami, Florida.

A waitress swooped to our booth, balancing an armful of pasta, breadsticks, and some icky green stuff people somehow enjoy (back then, in 2007, I certainly did not understand the allure).

"Tell me when," the waitress said to my wife, Mary, as fresh pepper fell from a wooden grinder.

"That's good," Mary said. Then the waitress peppered my four children's salads, each following their healthy mother's lead. But I was in the mood to eat like a king, no need to spoil my appetite with lettuce and tomatoes.

Our waitress slid my food across the table and said, "Careful, it's hot!"

My fettuccine alfredo looked like Italy on a plate. As a full-bodied Italian, it was my solemn duty to celebrate the old country by eating every last noodle. Celebrate I did. And because I enjoyed pushing heavy things around in the gym every week, I never felt too bad about indulging. I had grown up playing football, so lifting weights was a normal life rhythm.

Over the meal we talked about the vacation we were about to take. We were going on a road trip in an RV across Florida and southern Georgia, hitting springs, campgrounds, and coastline. This was a first for us. But the windshield time and exotic beauty of our state would do us good. I was excited. Mary was supportive, though not thrilled (as she'd practically grown up in a tour bus). The kids were indifferent. After all, as Christopher, our oldest and only son, pointed out, it would be difficult to play video games. Quite a summertime hardship for a teenager.

Mary was laser focused on getting settled in the condo we had just closed on a week before in Stuart, Florida, a quiet coastal town about a hundred miles North of Miami.

"We better get going!" Mary said, pushing her plate away. "We have plenty to do at the condo and *a lot* of shopping before we leave."

She tilted her head, looking at me for emphasis. Then, with full bellies, we pried ourselves out of the booth to leave. Before walking away, I grabbed one more breadstick.

"For the road," I said to Mary.

We loaded into our truck and headed north. And a couple of hours later we pulled in front of the condo. Mary jumped out, shooed the kids into my mother and father's condo that was right next door to ours (quite a nice feature), and we settled in for the evening. We had a big day ahead of us.

WELCOME TO FLORIDA

If you've never been to Florida in the summer, I can describe it to you in one word: humid. It's not just muggy—it's like the air thickens. You can take a shower, put on clothes fresh from the drier, and then be damp by the time you walk to your mailbox. Most native Floridians say you get used to it, but I think they must grow a pair of gills.

So the next morning, greeted by immediate mugginess, we scarfed down breakfast and set off on our whirlwind of a day. The kids crammed into the backseat: Stephanie, our eleven-year-old, who is most like her father; Lauren, our nine-year old who is much smarter than her father; Gaby, our seven-year-old who is cuter than her father; and Christopher, our fifteen-year-old who is most like his mother. Then, the girls dropped Christopher and me off at the RV rental place to pick up some camping gear and condo decorations.

After they pulled away, we walked onto the lot and stopped. I raised my eyebrows, taken aback. The RVs looked more like tour buses than I expected. This was also the first time I'd ever examined the many compartments and ports cluttering their twenty-five-foot-long sides.

A guy met us on the sweltering asphalt, then led us to our imposing vehicle. I assumed he'd just throw us the keys and we'd take off. However, that's not how it went down. He explained every hatch, compartment, and hose, inching us around the perimeter of the RV.

"This compartment doubles as storage and access to the electrical…" *Blah, blah, blah.*

One of my faults is impatience—but this was especially pronounced as we panted in the blistering heat. Then, after two hours of instruction, Christopher and I finally pulled out of the parking lot. My mind raced with checklists and details. But the more pressing issue was not taking out any mailboxes—or pedestrians—on the way to meet the girls back at the condo.

Driving an RV feels a lot like sailing a boat for the first time. You're not sure what you're doing. The thing feels big, slow, and unwieldy, and your blind spots are bigger than a barn door. Christopher and I both ducked reflexively when we drove beneath the first stoplights.

"Dad, are we gonna kill ourselves this week?" Christopher asked.

"That's not the plan, but I guess we'll find out, buddy!"

Our laughs were cut short as I dodged a white-haired lady puttering along in a Ford Taurus. Fortunately, we managed to snake our way home. I cringed thinking about an entire week driving this thing. But no time to worry about that. I had to figure out a place to park in this narrow lot.

The brakes squealed as we stopped. Chapter one of our epic family vacation had begun. Christopher and the girls played video games and watched movies at my parents' while Mary and I surveyed our condo. We had shipped a few pieces of furniture ahead of us. But we still had a long way to go before it resembled anything close to a home away from home.

Later in the evening, Mary and I ran to the store, shopping list in hand. Usually, I stick pretty close to her as, in times past, it had proven moderately dangerous to set her loose with a credit card! However, as we darted through aisle after aisle, I began to feel tired.

Mary had her arms full of picture frames and asked over her shoulder, "Steve, could you get me a shopping cart, please?"

Normally, I'd have already seen her struggling and grabbed one. But my body felt like it was filling up with concrete. So I pretended not to hear her. After a few more minutes of browsing, before she could ask me again, I said: "Mary, you go ahead and finish up, I just need to rest a minute."

She stopped and looked at me with surprise. "You look ashen, Steve. Are you okay?"

"Yeah, I'm fine," I said, "just tired from dealing with the RV and everything else. I'll be in the furniture area. Let me know when you're ready to go."

Then I drug myself over to a chair and sat down, exhaustion setting in. Sure, it was a busy season with everything going on at the church we pastor, closing on the condo, and now our RV extravaganza. But I've always been a high energy guy with plenty of capacity. This fatigue was strange, not at all my *modus operandi*. But we would soon find out, the worst was yet to come.

LAYING THE FOUNDATION

2007 was a pivotal year for Metro Life Church. We had started it as a family in 1997 and were now renovating a warehouse complex that would become our new church building. While building projects can be a tall order for fundraising, volunteer engagement, and logistics, God had blessed us with amazing people. The typical hurdles weren't an issue. When we needed funds, a few players from our NBA team, the Miami Heat, began to attend, caught the vision, and gave generously. When we needed hands to swing hammers, men in the church stepped up. While this season wasn't without its hardships, my story wasn't one of a burned-out pastor barely limping into a midsummer vacation. Metro had momentum and we were capitalizing on it.

We were laying a foundation for generations to come— literally and figuratively. I've often said that you won't judge my ministry or life by the buildings, church attendance numbers, fancy watches, designer suits, or any other metric. Instead, you'll judge me by how my adult children live their lives. It's still a bold claim—but I believe it with everything in me. And even with all of the moving ministry pieces, Mary and I diligently prioritized time as a family as well as inviting the kids into the work itself.[4]

---

[4] For more on what this looks like today, listen to our podcast "The Family Business" by visiting AlessiFamilyBusiness.com.

I believe God's design is for families to do ministry together. One of the best illustrations is a picture of Christopher standing in a hole during this building season. We had jackhammered out the concrete and shoveled our way further down so Christopher could lay prayer-filled letters and a Bible in the physical foundation of this new building. Scripture, prayer, and families doing God's work together are the pillars Metro Life Church is built upon. The area pictured is just outside of my office door. So every day I step out into the sanctuary, my first steps are on that very spot.

Life was full, but I thought everything was under control. However, it wasn't until Mary and I left the furniture store and headed back to the condo that I learned things weren't as solid as they seemed. And as we left, we got a call that the furniture movers would be there soon, waiting to deliver our furniture. So we raced back to beat them there, and on the way, the humidity gave way to a downpour.

Fatigue or no fatigue, I had to sprint from the truck up the stairs to pull our patio's large sliding glass doors off their tracks so the movers could fit everything in. I tugged the first one out of place, grunting.

"Do you need help with that?" Mary asked, concerned.

"I think I got it," I replied. But as I reached for the second door an uneasy feeling crept into my upper chest and left shoulder. I stopped to rub the area, thinking I strained a muscle.

I BELIEVE GOD'S DESIGN
IS FOR FAMILIES TO DO
MINISTRY TOGETHER.

"Steve, is everything okay?" Mary asked.

I sat down, but the pain intensified, and waves of nausea flooded my stomach.

I said, "Listen, I'm gonna go next door and use the bathroom. I think I just have some heartburn."

The kids were engrossed in a game and didn't notice me entering my parents' condo, sweating and clutching my stomach. I barely made it to the master bathroom before getting sick. I stood, trying to collect myself. But I winced as the pain moved from my left shoulder toward the center of my chest. It felt like an elephant had just sat on top of me.

And there it was. I knew what was coming. I looked at myself in the mirror and said, "No Lord, not now..." Job's words sprang to mind: "What I feared has come upon me; what I dreaded has happened to me."[5]

Real fear flooded my body. Not for me, but for Mary and the kids. Above every other role, I cherish the title of father. So I limped through the door in a half-run, half-stumble back to our condo. A focus and calm washed over me, like a fighter about to enter the ring against an opponent of unknown size. I didn't know what was about to happen, but I did sense I was entering the fight of my life. There was no place for panic. However, the situation was deathly serious.

With my children's laughter still ringing in my ears, I said as calmly as I could: "Mary, call 911."

So the fight began.

EVERYONE HAS A FIGHT

Life isn't easy. Change comes at you fast. Sometimes we can see a battle looming ahead, but other times it's an ambush. I've always been a fan of boxing and had plenty of "fight" in me. Fighters train to go in with both hands blazing. They learn how to punch, how to aggressively pursue their opponent, how to deflect and defend against every kind of attack, and even how to pace themselves throughout a bout. However, I've often wondered if anyone trains the fighter how to get up off the mat.

---

[5] Job 3:25 NIV.

A number of years ago, I had the opportunity to learn the answer. A friend (who just happened to own my favorite Italian restaurant) connected me with the International Hall of Fame boxer Ray "Boom Boom" Mancini.

I was preaching through a series called "The Champ Life." So, we arranged to have Ray come to speak to our men's group based on the sermons. What he said that night will stick with me forever: "It's the punch you never see coming that knocks you out."

Doesn't that ring true? Whenever you think you have things under control, watch out. The knockout punch is the one you aren't prepared for. Most hits you see. You block them, or you turn your cheek. They might hurt a bit, but they don't take you down. It's that uppercut out of nowhere that sends you sprawling to the ground.

THE KNOCKOUT PUNCH IS THE ONE YOU AREN'T PREPARED FOR.

Fighting through the knockout blow, disoriented, with stars spinning around your head is the hardest part. I'm not sure you can really train for this inevitable part of a fighting career. It seems like a mindset, an instinct to never stop and push through the pain, even as the referee is counting down. We all must dig deep to find the same will to rise.

If your heart's still beating, I believe you have that capacity.

We each have a headline fight—some of us have many. Maybe you're in the middle of that fight right now. I wrote this book to share my story of wobbling back to my feet and how my life changed because of it. I also wrote it in the hope that you will find inspiration to win your own fight.

Life's greatest lessons come from the journey of rising from flat on our face to standing upright again. They come from the mirror moments, like I had in my parents' condo, looking myself in the eyes, gripping my chest, and remembering what was really at stake—my family. They come from humbling yourself enough to see where you need to change and sow new seeds to reap a better harvest.

This is how I got smacked in the jaw, going from a happy Father's Day at an Italian restaurant to a surprise 911 call. I know you have a fight of your own. So let's enter the ring together and find the strength to get back up, fight the good fight, and finish well, no matter what haymakers life throws our way.

But that night, my match was just beginning.

Chapter
Two

Forty-Two Minutes That Changed My Life

Five men burst into our condo, paramedics responding to Mary's 911 call. Loaded with gear and grim expressions, they took instant command. I was shirtless, covered in sweat, and I had taken off my glasses, wedding ring, and watch because I knew what was coming.

One of the paramedics handed Mary a form to fill out in the kitchen, while another shoved a children's aspirin into my hand.

"Chew that!" he said.

My chest felt like it was in a vice grip. The men peppered me with questions, and I answered through labored breaths.

"Have you taken any Viagra?" they asked.

"No sir," I replied, "don't need it."

I winced a half-smile, but the joke fell flat. They were intense and this wasn't a laughing matter. What I didn't know is that just hours before these same men had arrived at another man's house. Only, instead of making jokes about Viagra, he said nothing, because that man had died.

Every year, about 800,000 people in the United States have a heart attack. These range greatly in severity, but on average, nine out of ten people survive a heart attack episode.

But there is a specific type of heart attack that leaves almost 90 percent of people dead from sudden cardiac arrest[6]... and this was happening to me right now.

I clutched my stomach and doubled over.

"Mary, get me a trash can!"

I felt like I was going to throw up again. But that was just the foreshock of the magnitude 10.0 earthquake happening in my chest. I was having a widowmaker, that rare breed of heart attack caused by 100 percent blockage of the left anterior descending artery, which almost always leaves its sufferers dead.

I seized up and hit the ground hard.

Mary later described how the men dropped to the floor around me and began immediate CPR. Through blurred vision, I barely remember laying on my back, seeing one of the paramedics hovering over me. I felt sharp jabs in my arm as another paramedic struggled to get an IV in my arm, as the sweat made it difficult to catch the vein.

Then I moaned as the first man hammer-punched my chest, knocking the wind out of me.

"What was that for?" I gasped.

---

[6] John J. Pierce, D.O. "Heart Attack Survival Rates." *Preventative Diagnostic Center,* 25 May 2022, https://www.pdcenterlv.com/blog/heart-attack-survival-rates/.

Every fiber in my body screamed. I couldn't breathe. My mind raced.

"Steve, this is going to hurt," another paramedic said.

I looked down and saw the paddles as he pressed them into my chest and said, "Clear!"

It felt like someone dropped me from a second-story balcony.

"Stay with us, Steve. Stay with us!" they urged me.

But their voices faded into white noise as I blacked out.

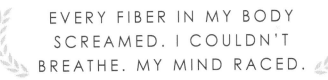

EVERY FIBER IN MY BODY SCREAMED. I COULDN'T BREATHE. MY MIND RACED.

FORTY-TWO MINUTES

Those men worked on me for forty-two minutes, hitting me with the paddles seven times. They told Mary that protocol was to stop after four, but they had never saved someone after a heart attack before. They were determined that day.

Forty-two minutes is a long time. It's a lifetime, when you think about what was going on. It was enough time for Mary to think about all the things that could happen as she watched them pump and beat and shock me over and over on our condo floor. The place that was supposed to be filled with years of happy memories was fast becoming my deathbed.

She began to pace in the kitchen, unable to do much more than say the name of Jesus over and over.

19

Prayer is our first response, not our last resort. It's a frontlines-of-battle activity.

One of the paramedics asked Mary to answer more questions, obviously trying to redirect her attention as the other four worked to keep me alive. She could tell they were close to giving up hope.

"Should I call someone?" she asked.

At just that moment, I woke up, hearing Mary's voice ring through the paramedic's intense words.

"Don't call my dad!" I said, before starting to fade again.

"Call everyone in your family," the paramedic told Mary. "Call everyone you want to call, let them know he's had a heart attack, and let them know we're working on him."

Mary could've asked, at that moment, if I was going to make it. It was the perfect invitation for the question. But she steeled herself and dialed the first person who came to mind, her best friend, confidant, and twin sister, Martha Munizzi.

"Martha," Mary said, "Steve is having a heart attack. And it's really, really bad."

Her sister, standing in the middle of an aisle at a Target, began to pray boldly. She declared God's power, goodness, and healing over me. That woman brought heaven into our room from hundreds of miles away. Prayer is our first response, not our last resort. It's a frontlines-of-battle activity. It is how God calms our storms.

"Mary," she said, "don't you dare waver. He's gonna live. You hold onto that. He will live and not die."

As if on cue, the paramedics stabilized me, prepping to move me. Mary began making more phone calls. The Lord gave her a strength she later said she couldn't have tapped into on her own if she'd tried. In all of the chaos, God gave her peace and calm, enabling her to manage the moment without becoming hysterical or giving up hope. She described it as the Lord showing her two doors, side by side: one marked life, the other death. And as she went next door to give my parents and our kids an update on what was going on, she heard God speak to her.

It's life or death, Mary. You choose.

It wasn't that she had the power in her hand to decide whether I lived or died, that she could sway the outcome. It was the power to choose life *until* I died. She could lose her mind in the moment or lean fully on God and let him be who he promised to be. She chose to side with life in how she prayed and communicated what was going on, until I took my last breath.

"God provided me with a gift in that terrifying moment. It was one of the greatest encounters with the Lord that I've ever had in my life," she tells people when we share our story.

Mary chose life. She embraced the better portion. She claimed God's promises. She didn't give even an inch to despair. Hope in the face of tragedy isn't foolishness, it is strength. And Mary was strong.

She went to talk to the kids. "Listen to me," she told them. "Dad's going to be alright. I don't want you to be scared."

She asked our fifteen-year-old son Christopher to stay there with the girls. "You're going to see Dad come out on a stretcher. You will not let the girls see, and you'll tell them that he hurt his back."

Christopher nodded, accepting his mission to step up as a man.

Back at our condo, as the paramedics prepared me for the move to the ambulance, Mary noticed a woman standing on the balcony across from ours. The woman could see everything that was happening.

Don't come over here, Mary thought when she saw the woman. That's unlike Mary, whose personality is very welcoming and kind, almost to a fault. But God was still at work, even if we didn't realize it at the time.

At the hospital, I was wheeled away, and Mary was left to sit in the waiting room alone. By then, everyone in the family knew. A former pastor and mentor of ours called her, and as she filled him in on the details, one of the paramedics walked into the waiting room with a female chaplain wearing some sort of a clerical collar. It was clear he intended for the chaplain to comfort Mary, but they had an expression on their faces that anticipated bad news, and she had the same feeling about the chaplain as she did about the woman on the balcony.

Don't come over here.

"I'm good," Mary told her, holding up her hand to stop them.

"Okay," the chaplain said. "I'm here if you need me." And then she walked away.

Still, Mary rejected any words or people that were not partnered with life. She still saw that door and knew her role was to hold it open.

THE DOOR OF LIFE

As a boy, I was a frequent flier in the emergency room. I grew up back in the era when kids got to play outside without hovering parents or smartphones with GPS trackers. Every summer, the neighborhood boys and I would hop on our bikes and rip around until evening. As long as I stayed within earshot of my mother's dinnertime call, I was alright.

However, one night when I was ten, I'd adventured a little further than usual for two reasons. First, because there was a large palm tree that a hurricane blew over. Its trunk now had the perfect slope to play ninja and see how far up you could climb. Second, there were girls hanging around the tree. Those were two great reasons to rustle up some trouble.

We'd pulled up on our bikes and I'd skidded to a stop, swinging my back tire wide and planting my foot down like Evel Knievel. We puffed out our chests and triple-dog-dared each other to make the climb. All the while, we took quick glances to see if the girls were watching. Sure enough, they were.

It was show time.

I'd gripped my feet into the earth like a stamping bull about to charge. I needed maximum traction to gain enough speed. Sure enough, I hit that tree running as fast as my little feet could carry me. And for one electric moment, my tread held onto the curved palm like a lizard. However, my ascent was over as quickly as it had begun. I lost my balance and toppled, grasping for the trunk but finding only air.

I landed with a thud and crack on my right arm. Tears welled up in my eyes, but I knew I couldn't cry in front of the girls. I had to play tough. But after a few minutes fighting back the waterworks, I gingerly sat back on my bike and rode home, my good arm controlling the handlebars.

My mom immediately knew something was wrong. And after I explained what happened, she and my dad scooped me up and brought me to the ER. As I sat on the bed, waiting for the doctor, my mom asked, "Stephen, why on earth did you try to run up that palm tree?"

"I'm so sorry," I said, "but I did it for the girls, Mom. I wanted them to see how cool I am!"

Even as I clutched my broken bird wing, my eyes twinkled with the thought of being the tough guy and impressing some girls. However, after forty-two minutes at death's door, I now found myself in another ER. Only this time, it wasn't me who impressed a girl; it was a woman, Mary, who impressed me. She kept my family informed and prayed, keeping a hold of that door of life.

I woke up, confused and nauseous. It took me a moment to realize where I was. Then I saw a doctor standing next to me and said, "I'm going to be sick..."

"Don't you throw up on my floor!" she barked. But it was too late. I threw up before passing out again.

My nausea was from the stent they were inserting to open up that clogged artery. It's a tiny mesh tube that acted as an open door for oxygenated blood to flow to the rest of my body—it did its job physically as Mary did hers spiritually. The door of life was open.

When they were done, the doctor brusquely called Mary back to where I was, in a cold room on a metal bed. I was hurting and confused, my chest radiating pain, and the demeanor of the doctor only added to the misery. They'd brought Mary in so I could see her before being taken to observation.

Mary walked over to me on that cold metal bed, where I was crying, and brought a sense of peace with her. The chaos of what had happened, and the unpleasant attitude of the doctor, had made everything dark. Mary had a different spirit

Even in the hospital environment, where the doctor may not have been partnering with life, God protected us by guiding Mary.

about her. Even in the hospital environment, where the doctor may not have been partnering with life, God protected us by guiding Mary. Where she went, she brought peace.

After I was wheeled away, Mary returned to the waiting room, which began filling with friends and people from the church. Dr. Vanessa Gordon, a missionary doctor and friend who was on her way to the hospital to be with Mary, called and asked if they'd put a stent in. Mary confirmed they had.

"You can relax," Vanessa told her. "The worst is over."

I am so thankful that Vanessa took the time to make that call to Mary, even though she could have waited until she arrived. The hospital hadn't told Mary much of anything, and she'd been holding onto life and hope with everything God gave her. Hearing that reassurance from Vanessa was a moment to exhale.

My parents showed up next. But when Mary told them that I was going to be okay, they didn't believe it.

"Don't lie to us," my mother said, her frail voice cracking. "Tell me the truth."

"No, no, I'm telling you he's fine," Mary reassured them. She could see the fear on my parents' faces, and my mother, who was deep in a battle with cancer, was so weak from chemotherapy it seemed as if bad news would wipe her out. Thankfully, it was true. I had survived an episode with a near 90 percent mortality rate.

YOUR 42 MOMENT

If you've ever been unconscious, you know how confusing it is. When you come to, you wonder: *Where am I? How did I get here? What happened?* When those paramedics hit me with everything in their bag, I had that physical moment of confusion. But I also had that moment in a deeper way because it made me take stock of my life.

"What did I do to deserve this, God?" I found myself asking. "Why do I need this in my life? What is the lesson here? Is it that I didn't protect myself well enough? Did I leave the door open to the devil? Is this a punishment? Or something else entirely?"

I HAD SURVIVED AN EPISODE WITH A NEAR 90 PERCENT MORTALITY RATE.

I didn't know how to respond to a hit like this other than to decide it was okay not to be immediately okay. I didn't have to know everything right now. I couldn't preach for the church because I couldn't even preach for me. I had to focus on regaining the strength to stand. And when you get hit in life, it doesn't have to make sense beyond that.

For forty-two minutes, those paramedics pounded the life back into me. Seven times, they hit me with those paddles. And may I tell you something? You will have a 42 moment. In fact, you probably already have.

It may not be a widowmaker or brush with death. But you will face tragedy, hardship, and odds that are lightyears from being in your favor.

A 42 is a moment of devastation so powerful you're unsure if you'll ever recover. It strikes with such force it is beyond

A 42 is a moment of devastation so powerful you're unsure if you'll ever recover.

a knockout punch—it is a death blow. It is an intensely painful moment or season you find it hard to believe you can survive.

For some, your 42 is a financial crisis that drops you to your knees. Fortunes that you once found so much stability in can evaporate overnight. Markets crash, business partners embezzle, empires of cash topple to the ground. Your 42 might be a shattered relationship. A marriage rocked by adultery, friendships ending in betrayal, strife and bitterness ripping your family apart. Your 42 could be a life-threatening illness. From cancer to COVID, our world teems with sickness and death.

We miscarry, losing precious children… Our 42.

We are tormented, trapped in mental health challenges… Our 42.

We struggle through infertility, longing for life we cannot have… Our 42.

We are paralyzed by fear, past traumas haunting us awake and asleep… Our 42.

We are isolated, stuck in cycles of shame, guilt, and addiction… Our 42.

We feel lost without a way home… Our 42.

What is your 42? The list is endless—so is the hurt. But my friend, my story is a testimony to this truth: If your heart's still beating, God's not finished with you. You are reading this for a purpose. And I hope you find strength in the pages ahead.

Jesus promised that this world will be filled with 42s, troubles of every kind. He also said, "But take heart! I have overcome the world."[7]

---

[7] John 16:33 NIV.

Life's darkest moments can give way to life's greatest blessings. But only if we look past our pain and fix our eyes on the path ahead. Only if we cling to the truth that the One who holds the universe holds us in the palm of His hand. And only if we resolve to climb back to our feet and finish well.

To be honest, though, I wouldn't have been that interested in hearing this as I sat in that sterile hospital room. I wouldn't have wanted to hear the Christian clichés. If you had read that encouragement to me, I may have even suggested you save those words for graduation cards and coffee mugs. But my promise, and my testimony, is that there is hope beyond the present pain.

 IF YOUR HEART'S STILL BEATING, GOD'S NOT FINISHED WITH YOU.

You can't expect to be normal right away. Broken hearts take time to mend and accomplishing the little things that become the big things takes work. It's a process. It was for me. Your 42 may be beyond anything I can imagine. But tomorrow, the sun will still rise and set, and God will still ask you to make a choice.

You can choose the door marked life or the door marked death.

Which will you open?

Chapter
Three

On The Ropes

I was in the ICU for almost a week. As a guy who hates sitting still for more than five minutes, this was agonizing. However, it wasn't so much the forced "rest" that bothered me—it was the reality that I *needed* it. I'd come face to face with my humanity and drank the bitter medicine of mortality. Even after being released, I was still reeling both emotionally and mentally from this seismic event.

What was life, ministry, and my future supposed to look like now?

A few days after leaving the hospital, I had to go back for a checkup. And wouldn't you know it, my doctor asked if we had a place where I could take it easy for six weeks.

"Frankly, what you guys do for a living is one of the highest stress jobs around," he told us, making sure we understood that we needed time away from our busy lives in Miami.

No need to convince me on that one. Any time you're working with people, you're bearing their burdens, and their pain can easily become yours if you're not careful. You're almost always meeting people at the toughest times of their lives.

"You need to get away from all of that for at least six weeks," the doctor said. "Otherwise, we'll see you back here— or worse."

The condo turned out to be a blessing. We had to reinvent our lives during that time and that's hard to do in an environment where your old habits were formed. Mary changed how we ate. Everything seemed like it was a salad or fish, straight off the heart-healthy list. French fries were evil, and big plates of pasta were out of the question.

It wasn't just our diet that changed, of course.

WE HAD TO RELEARN
HOW TO MAKE IT
THROUGH THE DAY.

We had to relearn how to make it through the day. Mary didn't want to leave me alone out of fear something would happen to me. She'd be in the same room when I was exercising. We'd leave the bathroom door open, just in case. Shock and trauma create a nagging spirit that starts to follow you, constantly whispering to you. *Don't let your guard down. Stay nervous. Stay afraid.* If she called out to me and I didn't answer her right away, she'd get anxious and search me out.

Forty-two minutes were long, but so were those six weeks.

BEING THE GUY ON THE OTHER SIDE

For six weeks, I came face to face with my weak humanity, and I felt completely lost.

As a pastor, I was the guy who made the diagnosis for others, who counseled them and helped them. I was the guy up front who took the heat, the one who did the helping and the leading. I took care of the church staff, of my family—not the other way around.

It was unsettling to have it all reversed, to be on the other side.

I had to watch my wife and everyone else take care of me. The church staff stepped in and did everything without me while friends came and cooked and cleaned at the condo. It felt as if my hands had been taken off of the rudder and familiar ground had been pulled out from under me; I was drifting without purpose.

Since my old work routine was out of the question, I had to figure out a new way to fill each day. The doctors had told me to do light exercise, and so Mary and I would go for walks around the condo to a bridge where we could look over the bay. Sometimes Mary couldn't go with me, and I felt so frail because I was afraid to go for a walk by myself. What if it happened again? Who would help me? How could I possibly be afraid to go for a walk?

One afternoon, while we were in the pool exercising, a woman got into the pool. It was the woman Mary had seen watching from across our balcony.

"Are you the couple that the paramedics came for a few weeks ago?" she asked.

As a church, we were growing. It's as if they saw that their leader was tired, and they had to hold up his arms.

"Yes," Mary said, but I could tell she was wary of where this was going. She felt very protective of me.

"I was on the balcony watching you that day," she said. "I just lost my brother, and he was the same age," she said, describing what was almost a parallel life situation to ours. Her brother had four kids, a son and three girls, just like us. He'd had a heart attack, just like me. But he was a larger fellow, his paramedics were different, and they couldn't save his life.

"My brother was the love of my life," the woman told us. "I don't know how I'll ever live without him."

I didn't know what to say. Here I was, a pastor used to giving comfort and encouragement, and I didn't know what to say because I was still trying to find my own footing with all that had happened.

For three months, I didn't go to church much because I felt so uncomfortable with my weakness. It was both beautiful and difficult to realize that the people Mary and I had poured into now poured into us. Just like Aaron and Hur held up Moses's arms so his staff would stay raised and the fight in the valley would be victorious, our friends and people from the church went above and beyond. As a church, we were growing. It's as if they saw that their leader was tired, and they had to hold up his arms. What Mary and I were experiencing, they were experiencing. They were going to walk through it with us.

David, a close friend in the ministry, had gone through a 42 moment of his own before my heart attack, and we'd become very close during those dark days. When Mary decided to attend a wedding during the six weeks recovery time, David said he'd come up and stay with me.

"Stay with me? I'm not a kid. I don't need a babysitter," I protested.

While I didn't like being alone, I was certainly going to try to get used to it. I had to. But I was overruled; they didn't want me to be alone that long. And in hindsight, they probably didn't want me to continue to wallow in isolation.

David decided we ought to go to a local course and play a round of golf. Normally I enjoy a day on the golf course, but I didn't feel like it that day. When life is upended or you feel lost, there's a strange conflict inside. You don't want to do much of anything, and you don't like that you're not doing anything. I liked golfing with David and always wanted to go before the heart attack, but now I was a different guy.

David was insistent, though, and soon we were out on the course. In the past, when I was "pre-heart attack Steve," we'd both enjoyed having a cigar while golfing. It was our tradition, but my old habits had to change. Sure, the green grass and the warm Florida sun and breezes were nice, but I had to stand there, with my golf club in hand, and watch him puff away on his cigar.

Standing there with a golf club but no cigar felt so wrong.

"I want a cigar," I said.

"Nope. You can't have one."

Add it to the list, that long, long list of post-heart attack can'ts. Can't be left alone, can't lift the weights I used to, can't do my job, can't eat that—and now I can't enjoy a cigar. I was a little annoyed.

We pulled up to the green in our golf cart. David set his cigar down on the cup holder, grabbed his putter, and began walking across the grass.

From high above us, hidden in a tree, a giant crow must have felt my pain. Like a sympathetic shadow, it swooped down and grabbed the cigar from the golf cart, barely dropping any ashes. It flew up to a branch and sat there, a smoking cigar hanging out of its beak, staring at us. If you'd slapped a pair of glasses on it, he could have been George Burns.

If Steve can't have a cigar, no one can have a cigar, it seemed to say. It was almost a thing of beauty.

"Are you kidding—" David said, looking up from the green while clutching his putter, seeing his cigar far above his head. To the horror of other golfers, we started throwing rocks at the crow until it finally flew away, cigar still in tow. We were both laughing pretty hard. It felt good, and relief rolled over me.

I can still laugh, I thought, breaking through that list of can'ts I'd found it easy to focus on. *My joy hasn't been taken from me. It's still there.*

It's too easy to keep track of what isn't normal, what isn't how it used to be, what isn't easy, what you can't do. Sometimes you need a crow puffing on a stogie over the putting green to put a smile on your face. Sometimes you need a friend to drag you out of the condo and onto the golf course.

David didn't babysit me that day. He didn't just take me out golfing. He helped reintroduce me to another round of life.

GUILT AND ISOLATION

When we experience life on the other side of what we're used to, it's confusing. We lose our bearings and have a tendency to isolate ourselves, pushing away what we should be pulling in. We make an enemy out of others real quick in these kinds of situations. We are uncomfortable with or resent needing help, even though God brings people alongside us to help us heal. We run from our local church instead of running to it. Substance abuse programs that take a support-group approach are correct that you need community when you're struggling; God never meant for you to do it alone.

Leaders, especially, can't be isolated. John Maxwell says that if you're a lonely leader, you're not leading correctly. If I'm alone too long, the enemy has way too much of a chance to trip me up; we need the checks and balances of accountability. Being alone must have a limit.

BEING ALONE MUST HAVE A LIMIT.

During those six weeks, I was forced to battle with both wanting isolation and knowing I needed others around me, operating not from a position of control, but of weakness. I was forced to consciously reset my routines, reset my habits, and think about what moving forward in life looked like now.

There is a recalibration that happens in the wake of a 42. As the dust settles, you grapple with what life is *supposed* to look like now. You may wonder if you're still the same person. Or, like me, you may even feel survivor's guilt that you lived when so many others facing your situation did not.

It's a strange cocktail of guilt and gratitude. And even though you cognitively understand you've done nothing wrong, you can't help but think of the thousands of widows who have lost husbands, children who have lost fathers, and parents who have lost children. Worse yet, there are those dealt the knockout blow of feeling entirely responsible for someone else's tragedy.

Remember famous boxer Ray "Boom Boom" Mancini who spoke to our men's group? Mancini held the World Boxing Association lightweight title from 1982 to 1984. He competed professionally from the late seventies into the early nineties. He knew what it was to take a punch in the ring but also in life.

In 1982, Mancini defended his title by defeating Korean boxer Duk Koo Kim in a brutal fight in Las Vegas. Both fighters pummeled each other, faces purple and swollen. The match lasted 14 rounds before a surprise left hook from Mancini sent Kim down. Moments after the fight ended, Kim collapsed from a blood clot in the brain, and died four days later.[8] The fallout from that moment was significant. Kim's son lost his father, and his wife became a widow. For a long time, Mancini struggled with depression and guilt, trying to come to grips with what had happened.

That was his 42. He obviously had done nothing wrong. But in the face of tragedy, good people grapple with guilt, grief, and isolation. However, like Mancini, and like me, you don't have to stay there.

---

[8] Kriegel, Mark. "A Step Back." The New York Times. The New York Times, September 17, 2012. https://www.nytimes.com/2012/09/17/sports/families-continue-to-heal-30-years-after-title-bout-between-ray-mancini-and-duk-koo-kim.html.

Whether you've experienced survivor's guilt or any other post-42 trauma, understand that these emotions don't mean you're broken—they mean you are poised to move ahead. They mean you are sorting through what your new life looks like. And this seems to be the path to recovery post-cardiac arrest *and* post-42 alike. It was for my dear friends, David and Paola, whose remarkable story teaches even as it inspires.

THE ANSWER ISN'T A NO, IT'S A HOW

David and Paola were high school sweethearts, in love from the start. After they married, they started attending Metro Life Church. Our church had many young couples that they became close to. Gradually, those couples began to have children.

But David and Paola, who had both come from humble backgrounds but now had successful careers, were going to wait a bit before starting their family. For five years, they built their relationship and enjoyed each other's company. They volunteered to help with the church kids' ministry and traveled extensively.

It was during a trip to Washington D.C. when things changed. While watching a young couple, close to their age, laughing and swinging their son between them, they both felt a pull at their heart. It was time to start a family, they were sure of it; and they announced their plans to the world.

End of the first year of trying, nothing happened.

End of the second year, still nothing.

By now, they were surrounded by friends and family members who were having kids and growing their own families. They celebrated those happy times with them, but there was also pain. As the years clicked by with no children of their own, they decided to visit a doctor to see what was wrong. They tried medication and all kinds of tests, but the final diagnosis was that they could not have children.

David and Paola had gone into that year of the diagnosis with hope, having no idea what was coming. And not only were their dreams of a family dashed, David's job as an architect ended. Out of nowhere, that punch they hadn't seen coming had landed and everything seemed to collapse.

I asked David to come on staff at the church. Initially he turned me down because he didn't want to work at a church as a "fallback" option, but Paola thought otherwise.

"Maybe God is inviting us to be a part of something special," she told him.

As it turns out, He was. David joined our team, and within the year, he was ordained and became part of our team of pastors, overseeing missions, outreach, and the remodel of the sanctuary. And even though David had put the idea of having a family on the backburner in the midst of all that transition, I knew the dream was still there.

While meeting David for coffee one afternoon, I put him on the hot seat. "You and your wife are special. You have amazing hearts," I told him. "You think you and your wife can't have a family, but you can."

When you're in a 42 moment, you want to hear people believe in a miracle for you. You want them to pray you through to the victory you envision, the original dream. You don't want to hear that you can be a miracle for someone else.

But that's what I told him. There were children out there who needed families. David and Paola could be their miracle.

We connected them to a ministry that provided homes for babies whose mothers wanted them to live instead of choosing abortion. They started the long process of becoming a licensed adoptive family, taking classes, gathering character references, and creating a family profile for the mothers to choose from. It seemed their plan was locked into place, and that the next stop was adopting a baby.

Maybe those out-of-the-blue hits are a surprise because we keep thinking we know what God ought to do next. For David and Paola, God had something else in mind. A young boy named James was in desperate need of a place to stay because of a difficult situation in his home. It involved going to court and asking that he legally be placed in David and Paola's home in foster care for a month.

Then it became three months. Then it was indefinite. Then they became a licensed foster care home. And then, within a few years, they added an infant girl to their foster family, who they were eventually able to adopt.

They did not have their own biological children. They had years of watching others around them grow their families. They didn't even get an infant from the ministry they'd applied to. It might seem as if God dropped a series of no's and closed doors in their path each time they asked for something. But did He? When it came to having a family, the answer was never a no. Instead, it was a question of how.

God, why did You allow this to happen to me? suddenly becomes *God, how can I partner with You through this?* The last question is full of infinite possibilities from an infinite God.

It might seem as if God dropped a series of no's and closed doors in their path each time they asked for something. But did He?

Have you made that mistake? Are you down for the count, on your back gasping for air, so sure that God gave you a no, so sure you could hear the door slamming shut, when instead, He was giving you the opportunity to work *with Him* through the how?

I like to ask people a question that seems simple on the surface but actually cuts to the core of this kind of moment: what is the next season of your life gonna be about?

There's no better time to ask it, there's no better opportunity for change, than when you're in a 42 moment and God is bringing you to the other side.

Chapter Four

Blind Spots

Just ahead of me on the road was a fifteen-passenger van filled with kids from the youth group and another adult from the church driving. We were all heading to Disney World for a fun youth day. I was following the van in my own car, with my girlfriend at the time next to me, and my sister, Debbie, in the back seat. I thought it would be a nice drive and a chance to chat with my girlfriend while I was home on college break, but Debbie had different ideas. It seemed she wanted to annoy me in front of my girlfriend, so she started kicking the back of my seat and wouldn't let up.

Keeping a grip on the steering wheel, I cranked my head towards the back seat. "Knock it off—" I started to say, but then I saw her. Debbie was having a seizure, and when I turned, I could see her eyes rolled back and her head was jerking. What I thought was kicking was her feet smacking against the seats and door. She was going to hurt herself.

I quickly pulled the car to the side of the road and yanked on the emergency brake. I hopped into the back seat and prayed. I knew you should never put your fingers in the mouth of someone having a seizure, but in a panic—and out of concern she'd bite her tongue—I shoved my fingers in her mouth.

While I was trying to comfort her and pray, she bit down hard on my fingers. Blood started to squirt everywhere, and the pain was intense. I didn't lose any fingers, but it felt like I would. While Debbie has outgrown her seizures, to this day, when I think of a seizure, I think of that bloody mess.

That's the picture that always comes to mind. Many years later, I had little girls of my own who were about Debbie's age when her seizures presented.

One evening, Mary and I were in our living room when we heard screaming upstairs. We sprinted to the commotion. And our daughter, Lauren, burst from the bathroom in a panic.

"What happened, Lauren?" Mary asked, holding her shoulders to comfort her.

"I—can't—remember," she said between heaving breaths. "I woke up—on—the shower floor."

She evidently passed out and then came to. It was concerning, but she seemed okay. No harm done, so we let it go. A few weeks later, as we were getting ready for church, we heard more screams—this time from our youngest daughter, Gaby. (These outbursts were becoming a thing.) Mary and I charged upstairs just in time to see Lauren convulsing on the floor, where she'd collapsed.

Lauren's body continued to jerk uncontrollably, and I saw that she had her foot stuck under the vanity. Blood was oozing out from a cut that grew larger with each spasm. I got on the floor and tried to move her foot, but her body was too stiff. I knew I'd hurt her if I kept at it.

It's just like Debbie, I thought. My fingers almost hurt thinking about it but not as much as it hurt to see Lauren bleeding, me helpless to do much of anything.

I called 911, something we were getting good at. When the paramedics showed up, they asked if she had epilepsy. We told them no.

A month later, it happened again, and we knew something was seriously wrong. The doctor agreed, and just like me with my heart attack, Lauren had to change her lifestyle. New medication. Paying attention to any trigger imaginable—from diet to hot showers. As I well know, such radical change is no small thing.

We had had no idea that anything was wrong with Lauren. We had no idea that the same incidents would repeat themselves months later; only this time, it was Lauren who found Gaby unconscious and limbs convulsing.

Debbie, Lauren, Gaby. Apparently, this runs in the family. It caught us completely by surprise. We had a blind spot. And of course, the trouble with blind spots is that you don't know you have them. They are punches you don't see coming.

So many things demand our attention, making blind spots hard to notice. Sometimes, they come from out of the blue, like those seizures. Other times, there are prophetic precursors that reveal what the future may have in store. Like dark storm clouds on the horizon, they signal trouble is a-comin'. The problem is, they're often far away, too far to worry us. After all, maybe they'll miss us altogether.

So many things demand our attention, making blind spots hard to notice.

The trouble is, if we don't take a serious look at our lives, and where our actions (or inactions) are taking us, we can end up in a world of preventable pain. Trust me, while I'm a preacher, I'm not preaching *at you*. Rather, I'll invite you to a fireside chat I should've had with myself before the 42 moment ever hit me.

SURPRISE, SURPRISE

Before my heart attack, my life was full of distraction. Church building projects, a new condo, an RV vacation—all of that on top of the already high demands that come with ministry, marriage, and family.

Even if I wanted to actively look for potential blind spots, when would I find the time? I got so busy with Big Things that I had to take on a triage mentality, and what I thought were little things I let slide.

Who knew that food was a Big Thing?

Because that's what food was: it was my blind spot. Food helped me with all of those stressors that I didn't even realize were happening. Like all of us, I knew I had to do better with my health, but it turned into a next-month project because this month was already overfilled.

"I'll just have this plate of fettuccine tonight, and I'll do better tomorrow," was my approach. Kicking the can down the road seemed to work, though the reality is that the blockage in my arteries probably started happening in my twenties and thirties. But back then, my only health metric was that my chest should stick out further than my stomach.

In my forties, though, my stomach was winning the race against my chest. I wasn't able to hit the gym as I had when I was younger because life was busier. Mary and I started to do some cardio exercise in the park, but I still kept up eating and using food to deal with stress. The eating gave me comfort, and I thought I was covered because I was still doing the exercise part.

You'd like to think you'll have a heads-up before that blind spot punch lands square on your jaw.

Up to the day of my heart attack, I had no physical warning anything was wrong. Sure, my doctor had warned me about high blood pressure and other things. And yes, I didn't have the energy I had when I was younger. But everyone slows down a bit as they get older, right? I was fine, and normal, for my age.

Fine, that is, until those forty-two minutes on the floor.

Before having a stent placed in my artery, the increasing blockage kept blood from flowing well, which unknowingly decreased my energy. What I chalked up to "getting old" was really reduced blood flow in my body. Within a month or two after the stent, I had higher energy levels. My mind was sharper. More oxygenated blood was delivered to my brain and body.

As someone who likes to take a lesson out of everything, I was searching for a reason for everything that happened that day and in the aftermath. In the hospital, I remember flipping through the years of my life like a photo album, trying to find the lesson God wanted me to learn. To me, there are order and meaning behind everything 99.9 percent of the time.

Somewhere, a principle lurked. So, what was it?

When my family came in to see me at the hospital right after the attack, the first words out of my mouth were, "I'm sorry."

I'd almost left the people I love the most alone because I couldn't put down cheeseburgers. My blind spot almost killed me. All because I didn't follow the most foundational principle of all: sowing and reaping.

Physically, I reaped what I had sown. I planted bad seeds that ended up hurting the people I loved. I had lived with an unchecked blind spot that almost claimed everything. I had been hurtling toward death at 100 miles per hour and hadn't even known it.

MY BLIND SPOT ALMOST KILLED ME.

WHEN YOU GET A BAD HARVEST

We have a family farm in Southern Georgia. That is my happy place. Over the years we've built a 6,000-square-foot "barnatorium" with living space, a commercial kitchen, and a vaulted great room. Multiple times per year, we host men's retreats with our Goodfellas group. It's a slice of heaven. However, even for its perfection, we still get a bad harvest in our fields now and then. There are all kinds of reasons you get a rotten harvest—soil, weeds, disease, insects, weather, seeds—and while some of that you can't control, much of it you can. What you plant and allow in the soil can give you either a bountiful or blighted harvest.

Years back, there was a couple in our church who wanted me to marry them. Every pastor knows that sinking moment where you're asked to marry someone, but you know that you can't. People who insist they are in love are rarely able to hear your reasons why; it's nearly always confrontational and emotional. But as a pastor, I had to speak up.

"You shouldn't marry him," I told the young woman after I said I couldn't marry them. I knew her boyfriend to be a bit of a hustler, unable to keep a job but always full of talk and chasing the next best thing. That kind of a lifestyle takes the same approach towards relationships, too, and sooner or later it would come around and visit their marriage. Plus, they were already living together. I couldn't marry them under those conditions.

I'd like to tell you that she listened to me, but she did not. They insisted I was wrong, they were in love, and were going to follow their heart. They chose to leave the church, blaming me for not supporting them, and finding someone else who would marry them. In a few short years, they were divorced. He was quickly remarried to another woman in New York, doing the same thing all over again to someone else.

Sometimes the seed seems good, and the effort seems worthwhile, but the harvest reveals a different truth.

I recently watched the HBO film *Tony Hawk: Until the Wheels Fall Off*. The filmmakers captured the skateboarding legend's attempt to do a tricky move that had three full rotations, a 1080. The amount of times he failed was spectacular (and painful to watch), but he was determined to stick the landing. He'd crush his ribs; his helmet would fly off and he'd hit his head; groggy and sore, he'd be laid out with his board

Sometimes the seed seems good, and the effort seems worthwhile, but the harvest reveals a different truth.

off in the other direction—but he wouldn't stop. He was going to get it right. Even if he seriously hurt himself or caused permanent physical damage to his brain or his body, it was 1080 or bust. And he was going to stick that landing.

And he did. He nailed the 1080, and while it was quite a moment, it was clear he wanted to move on from it.

Yeah, he was the first to land a 1080, but it had caused him so much pain and so many injuries and setbacks that he wondered if it had been worth it. That 1080 cost him something he wasn't willing to keep paying the price for, even as other skateboarders managed to pull it off after he set the pace.

"But Tony, we got to see you do it first!" people might say, trying to convince him it was a good harvest.

"But look what it cost me."

SOMETIMES WE DON'T REALIZE THE FULL PRICE OF OUR PURSUIT.

I get it. Sometimes we don't realize the full price of our pursuit. We determine something is so important, and we sow into it everything we've got. Then, when we finally get to the end and we're worn out, we realize the price was way too high. I often ask my business friends how much is enough. How much sacrifice is acceptable, when you're sacrificing your marriage, your faith, or your kids? How much is money and fame really worth? You finally landed that 1080, and the world can see your success. But what did it cost you?

Sometimes the seed is good and, in a different season of life, your harvest would be great. But your timing is off. Farmers know that there's a limited window to plant. There's a proper order for planting and harvest. Each crop comes with a defined season, and you learn what crops should be planted after another. First plant the legumes to get the nitrogen in the soil. Then plant the corn. Sometimes you need to leave the ground fallow to regenerate.

The most difficult harvest is when something happens that you can't control. On a trip out to our farm, I saw that the pigs had gotten into the corn and nearly destroyed it. Not much could be done about it at that point beyond harvesting what was left, getting the pigs out, and sowing new seed for the next round. You can't change what is, only what will be.

I got to thinking how believers tend to get the idea of harvest wrong. We want to blame the devil when we have a bad harvest in our lives.

"It was a good crop until those pigs got into it!" we say, pointing the blame at the pigs.

You can curse the pigs all you want, but it won't change the harvest.

Like David in Psalm 51, we have to own what we harvest. Whether it was because you planted the wrong seed at the wrong time, or the pigs got in, you'll never have a new harvest until you start sowing new seed.

It takes time for something new to take root and grow into a harvest. But the reason God is big on repentance and changing what we value is because He knows we have to start sowing something different. We can't keep crying about the pigs. When I get a bad harvest at the farm, I'd be insane to think

It takes time for something new to take root and grow into a harvest.

the harvest is going to be better next year if I don't make some adjustments.

My heart attack was a really bad harvest, and it got me thinking about how I missed seeing all the bad seeds I was planting during those years of free-for-all eating, where I thought a little exercise would offset an all-you-can-eat buffet. I was sowing awful seed and thought it wouldn't catch up to me, allowing a blind spot to take root.

"Why didn't you tell me, God!?" I could say, angry fist to the sky, mixing blame with "why me?" But God is gracious enough to give us a choice of what we'll plant.

If I could give my kids one gift, it would be to tell them one thing: focus on the seed that you're sowing right now. Make sure it's godly, quality seed.

When you grasp the concept of sowing and reaping, you start to take hold of wisdom. Godly wisdom is what keeps you out of the ditch that deliverance needs to pull you out of. If you walk in godly wisdom and follow godly principles, you don't have to keep showing up for the prayer line for the same things every Sunday.

"I need prayer because my marriage is on the rocks."

"I need prayer to beat this addiction."

"I need prayer because my debt is more than I can handle."

Yes, we have needs, and there are things out of our control. Hurricane Andrew does hit. Drought or hail can come out of nowhere and destroy your carefully planted and weeded field. But as a Christian, when do you start being the guy who prays for others rather than being the guy everyone has to constantly pray for? When will you finally open a different bag of seeds and follow good principles?

PRINCIPLES ARE MEANT
TO BE FOLLOWED

Our church has a leadership cultural covenant (LCC), which is closely aligned with our culture and principles.

To be fair, nothing about the LCC is sexy. However, I knew we had to help our people succeed spiritually at church—and it would start with our leadership. The LCC grew out of that soil; we didn't want that to happen again, so the idea was to use it to make sure the staff were aligned with those principles as well. If someone was heading for a cliff, we wanted to find out and bring them back to safety.

The staff was a little nervous at first. Sitting down with someone else and asking them, on a scale of one to ten, how they were doing with each area covered in the LCC was going to be confrontational and prying, no matter how you approached it. The idea wasn't to create fear and shame but to let staff be honest. If there was an area where you were below a five, we would pray with you about it and keep you accountable.

That first year was basically an introduction of the idea to our teams. There was a reluctance to adopt it, perhaps because the idea was intimidating and new. The second year, we tried to get more intentional.

"Let's remember why we're doing this," I told the team, reminding them it was about spiritual success and not to be threatening or intrusive.

But then, in 2020, the pandemic struck. If we'd had a solid foundation with the LCC going into that year, I don't think we'd have lost as many people during that time; and we certainly wouldn't have found ourselves operating in survival mode.

When 2021 rolled around and life started to swing back to normal, we attempted to come back to the LCC. I've read that it takes about three years to make real change in an organization, but my get-er-done nature meant I was seriously exasperated. Adoption of the LCC was dragging like a turtle crawling through molasses.

Soon we were into 2022. My daughter helped change the LCC up a bit by adding some coaching to our yearly staff retreat. I took the staff through a Zoom call where I used the LCC on my own ministry assistants so they could see what it would look like.

No joy.

"Guys, what's going on here? Nobody's doing the LCC," I said, giving them a deadline to complete it with their own staff. "I'm telling you to do this. It's not a suggestion."

Two weeks later, at a staff meeting in which I listened to several people explain how they'd like to change things, I asked who had used the LCC because it was a fit for our culture and would reveal whether or not staff were in tune with our core principles.

No one raised their hand.

"You want to change something, and you haven't even used it yet?" I asked. I ratcheted up the deadline and gave them seven days to put the LCC to work.

In a way, the LCC revealed some seeds planted in our church that we weren't aware of. The reluctance to use it was revealing on its own. We ended up losing some precious people, some who had been with us for years before the LCC was in place. These were people who were very up-close and personal to me, some I'd known their entire lives. Like a doctor giving an exam, the LCC is what reveals if there are any potential problems.

Principles are meant to be lived by. I would rather lose a working relationship with someone than contradict our church principles. That's not a small thing for me to say as I place a very high value on relationships. But I value our church principles more because they are foundational. You compromise on principles, and pretty soon you have a wreck.

YOU COMPROMISE ON PRINCIPLES, AND PRETTY SOON YOU HAVE A WRECK.

The same can be said for our personal lives. We all have certain principles. I had my own, but my heart attack grew out of me not following them and ignoring my doctor.

WHAT DO YOU MEAN MEDICATION?

In my early forties, my doctor had suggested medication for high blood pressure, but I chose to ignore it.

My dad had been on blood pressure medications since his thirties, and I hated that. However, nothing ever happened to him, so I figured I could simply work harder and avoid relying on them. I didn't like the idea of taking medication because I thought that was for sick people. In a way, I wanted to declare—in faith—that I was healthy.

And that's great, until you almost drop dead except for forty-two minutes of resuscitation.

I had a new life after that, one that was full of pills (though I'm off of most of them by now). My diet went from being a meat, bread, and potatoes guy to swimming in salads. I saw a cardiologist about as much as I saw my golf clubs. You can either live according to your principles or die with them in view.

Realizing how much of this was my own doing made me feel shame, even though I was still so grateful that God was giving me a new chance at life. In fact, the three things I felt the most were shame that I hadn't kept to my principles, gratitude to God for life, and...guilt.

I'm talking about survivor's guilt, something both Mary and I struggled with after my heart attack. How strange to feel both intense gratitude *and* guilt for being alive, for surviving a kind of heart attack that kills nearly 90 percent of people.

You cling to faith to overcome the fear that the hammer might drop.

You cling to faith to fight the guilt that the hammer didn't drop.

You cling to faith to process the intense gratitude that you serve a God who doesn't drop hammers.

That survivor's guilt made it difficult to share our story. We knew there were many whose loved ones had died, many whose situations hadn't been orchestrated as ours was.

The neighbor whose brother died in a nearly identical situation.

The man installing my generator who died from a heart attack.

That we were at the new condo in Stuart instead of in Miami-Dade County, where paramedic response time is slower.

How strange to feel both intense gratitude and guilt for being alive, for surviving a kind of heart attack that kills nearly 90 percent of people.

That my paramedics had lost a man to a heart attack earlier in the day and were determined to save me.

"We heard your wife on the phone, calling and praying with people," they told me. "We figured you were somebody special, and we wanted to save you."

How do I talk about being pulled back from the jaws of death when I can't tell someone why they can't say the same? We almost felt guilty about God's grace.

Whether it's a heart attack or something else where you lived while others died, you'll feel survivor's guilt. For me, I can't tell you why or why not. What I have is forty-two minutes.

I can tell you that I planted bad seeds, I didn't live according to my principles, I allowed a blind spot to grow, and God gave me forty-two minutes to catch up. Because, from His view, there was no blind spot.

In Mark 10:46–52, Jesus walked by a blind beggar. He knew what the man wanted, but he asked anyway.

"What do you want me to do for you?" Jesus asked.

In John 5:1–9, we read about a man who had been disabled for 38 years. When Jesus came by and saw him, he knew what his problem was.

"Do you want to be healed?" Jesus asked.

If you're like me, you have blind spots. You've planted bad seeds, even if the harvest hasn't come in. Do you want to see, to be healed?

My prayer is that my 42 moment doesn't have to be yours. That you can hear my story and you won't have to go all the way down to the floor and taste death before you answer Jesus with a resounding "yes!"

Why did I live?

I don't know. But I have more time because of it, and I don't want to waste it on anything but pointing people to the God who stepped in and saved my life during those forty-two minutes.

Chapter Five

Running With A Limp

Running and I are not on good terms. I'll never run a marathon, and I'm not crying about that. You will not see one of those 26.2 stickers on the back of my car.

My dad wasn't a sports guy; his focus was on building the church. But football is a big deal in the south; and as a kid, I remember begging my mom to let me play little league football. I had two sisters. I pushed them around easily enough. How hard could football be?

As it turns out, pushing your sisters around was completely different than getting pummeled by a bunch of boys out on the playing field. It didn't take long for me to start to hate playing football because I was intimidated, and the running was awful.

I was overweight—"hefty" as my mom would say ever so kindly—and the physical exercises demanded of us during practice were too much. Practice was torture with its drills and sprints; and by the third practice, I was done with the football thing. Done, forever. I was prepared to watch it on TV, but that's it.

The turning moment came at the end of practice. The coach had us, already exhausted, finish out the day by running sprints. I was about ready to puke, and it wasn't long before the other boys were finishing their sprints while I was still chugging along out on the field. What I was doing was less a sprint and more a straggle.

"Come on, preacher boy!" the coach screamed at me at one point, since I was the last one still running. "Come on! You can make it!"

I'm surprised my heart didn't give out right there, as a kid. I miraculously managed to wheeze and gasp my way through to the end.

"I'm never playing football again," I announced to my parents when they came to pick me up. "Coach made fun of me and called me 'preacher boy'."

Dad needed no further convincing. It didn't hurt that he wasn't thrilled to have to drive me to practice in the first place. From then on, my tackles and great plays were done against my sisters in and around the house. And even though I got into weightlifting and working out at the gym as I got older, the whole running thing was never me.

Walking around the hospital, in those early days after the heart attack, felt like a marathon; just getting out of bed was exhausting. But cabin fever had set in, there were no visitors to distract me all the time, and I wanted to get out of my room and look around.

"Are you alright, Mr. Alessi?" the nurse at the nurse's station outside of my room asked. I must have looked quite a sight, standing in the doorway in my hospital gown and standard issue gray booties. To be fair, I had tried to shave and clean up a bit before emerging from my room.

"Yes," I said. "Is it okay for me to take a walk?"

"Sure, just don't go too far," she said.

Down the hallway I went, slowly making my way. Just a week earlier I could've breezed down that hallway, but now it was a real workout. When I was past all of the other rooms, I started to cry. I felt pretty good at first; getting out of bed was proof I wasn't going to be an invalid, which was reassuring. But each step made me exponentially more tired, and it reminded me that life was going to be completely different from that moment on.

I had to make changes, some of which I knew I needed to make and some that I was going to be forced to make. No matter how sweet the American Heart Association dietician was, her visits were never a happy time. Certain foods had brought me comfort and calm, food with tastes and textures I loved; and now they were being taken away from me and replaced by meh.

With tears on my face, feet shuffling across the tile floor, I was quickly exhausted and knew I needed to get back to my room to rest. Turning the corner at the end of the short hallway felt like I'd run that marathon. Somewhere there was a coach yelling "come on, preacher boy!"

The return to my room was much slower, and I was breaking out in a sweat.

This is the day a walk down the hallway nearly took me out, I thought; and reality hit like a brick. From here on out, I was going to have this wound. The scars from the heart attack

The scars from the heart attack might not be visible after a while, but I knew that damage was there.

might not be visible after a while, but I knew that damage was there. I'd never forget what had happened to me; and if I wasn't careful, fear and anger would grow instead of positive change.

We all have some kind of wound, some kind of limp. You can let it put you on the sidelines where you'll just sit down for good, dwelling on how unfair life is, or you can get up and walk and maybe even learn to run with it. I think I've established my distaste of running pretty well, but I'll be honest: I'd never had any interest in running a marathon, until I was told I couldn't run one.

What do *you* do, when you have a permanent injury to your body or your spirit, some kind of limp? Do you go forward despite it, or let life pass you by?

AN ELITE STENT CLUB

I'm a card-carrying member of the prestigious Stent Club.

No joke—a heart stent comes with its own ID card. You're supposed to keep it on you at all times because it details important information about the stent, such as what type of stent was put in, its size, and what blood vessel it was put in. The idea is that any paramedics or doctors doing future medical procedures need to know that information so they can make the best decisions. It's kind of like those medic-alert bracelets that warn of serious allergies or medical conditions.

As it turns out, most people forget to carry that card around with them. Maybe they think it's not a big deal because a stent is so small. A stent is the size of an earphone wire. It's really,

really tiny. In my case, after they did an angioplasty to enlarge the blood vessel, they put the stent in through my groin.

You expect something that small to do something as big as keep the vessel open so blood can flow, and you have questions. At least, I did.

"Does this thing fail? What happens when it gets old? Does it get rusty?" I asked. Time hadn't done my body any favors, so surely it wouldn't do the stent any favors, either. "What happens to this thing over time?"

In time, I became fixated on cleaning out my arteries in case there was other blockage, and also to ward off any problems with the stent. Miraculously, I even developed a bit of an obsession for eating any and all green vegetables to help the process along.

Concern over the stent and what was going on led me to a doctor who offered alternative therapies, including chelation therapy. It's a therapy that uses what are called chelating agents, via an IV drip, to remove heavy metals from the body. I did thirty treatments, smelled like a vitamin dispensary, and had great peace of mind that it was helping clean out the plaque.

Chelation, green vegetables—it was like someone had flipped a switch, and the changes I had to make in life became easier when I viewed it in terms of not abusing my Stent Club status. Knowing I had a stent was a contradiction in feelings. It made me feel old, but it gave me some peace. It was so tiny that I was motivated to keep my arteries clean.

None of this was part of the plan I had for my life, prior to the heart attack. In my mind, the race I'd run would be a bit smoother. But here I was, realizing I'd be running it with a limp.

WRESTLING WITH GOD

Jacob was all alone, in the dark of night, when he had the wrestling match of his life.

We read of it in Genesis 32, how Jacob settled down for the night near the edge of a stream. He'd sent his family and possessions to the other side, and shortly after, a Man came along and started to wrestle with him.

Jacob wasn't going to give up easily. All night long they wrestled, and when the sun was just about to come up over the horizon, the Man touched the socket of Jacob's hip, permanently wounding him and giving him a limp for the rest of his life. Even in the pain, Jacob wouldn't let go, he wouldn't quit, until he got a blessing.

Wrestling with God usually looks much different, compared to what Jacob went through that night. In the days and weeks and months after the heart attack, I wrestled with God. And while I'm not saying that God outright reaches down and gives us our limp, I do want to emphasize that Jacob's limp didn't mean he was weak. It simply meant he wasn't as strong and as big as God.

Maybe that limp humbled Jacob a bit because Jacob wasn't a great guy. He had a personal history that lacked character and integrity. But when God was done with Jacob, he made a covenant that went far beyond Jacob's significant failings. God would still use him to carry out His bigger plan, despite the failures and flaws in Jacob. Even in our weak, frail, and damaged state, God will use us.

It doesn't mean you'll feel victorious. Victory through strength is the human approach, not victory in weakness. You can come out scarred and with a limp, feeling broken after wrestling with life. But God's strength is made greater in our weakness. His glory is seen through our limp because what He accomplishes in our lives is clearly because of His power, not our own.

Walking down the hospital hallway left me feeling weak and helpless and in tears. If this was just about humanity and what I could do in my own strength, I'd have never made it to today. Knowing that God's plan is so much bigger, knowing that I could wrestle with Him over it all and still come out the other side being used by Him, got me through then and still does today.

GOD'S STRENGTH IS MADE GREATER IN OUR WEAKNESS.

I mean, I failed the cheeseburger test. I didn't take care of myself. I didn't do what was needed to avoid the heart attack. I dropped the ball. But God picked it up because there was still more He had for me to accomplish. He didn't see an unusable specimen, broken and lying on the floor of the condo, getting hit with the paddles to stay alive. He saw how great His power would be demonstrated in my life with my broken body. He had a plan, though I didn't know it.

Knowing that is one thing. Feeling it is another.

In a way, not knowing God's plan ties into the survivor's guilt. When Mary and I were asked why I was allowed to survive and others didn't, the uncomfortable answer is…we don't know. God knows. God has a plan. We just don't know all the details, all the reasons.

If you can grab ahold of that—really grasp that you just can't know the why—then you eventually get to the right question you should be asking yourself. It's not "Why did this happen?" but "What will I do now?".

The journey to get from the first question to the second question is pretty long, practically a marathon. *Why God?* can turn into *Why not?* and then *What for?* and maybe even the horrible speculative *What if?* There's lots of room for anger and frustration and guilt in all of those questions. That's part of wrestling with God.

I'm a bit direct and not known for having the gift of counseling; but if you're wrestling with God about something, here's how I'd break it down.

You start by acknowledging it happened. Even if deep down, you know why it happened or what you did to cause it—like being the cheeseburger king—you have to accept it happened and you might not have all the answers as to why. This is less easy if you're the innocent victim of something horrific because there is zero hint at why something happened. But we can all acknowledge what happened, no matter how much of the "why" we understand.

From there, you really start to wrestle. Because now you have to decide how you'll respond. It happened, so now what?

Do you stop living and forever sit on that moment as the definition of who you are? Do you still trust the bigger picture? Do you grasp that something awful didn't take you out, even though it could have? What change could you make so it doesn't have to happen again? These kinds of life-changing moments are like flashing lights and sirens in your life. From this moment on, you'll be able to tie what you do going forward on back to that moment, that crossroads.

If you decide this won't happen again, what are you going to do about it? What do you have faith for? Can you start that business again, but better? Can you get to a place where you can love and trust again? Do you have faith a new door will open? Do you believe there is life after this, and you're going to have to live it?

Life is a precious miracle. It's too precious to discard. What a shame to survive something only to give up afterwards, letting your life dwindle to nothing on the sidelines, instead of wrestling through to daybreak with God.

God is right there with you. He doesn't allow something to happen to you that you and He can't bear together. He won't allow us to be tempted without giving us a way to escape.

Growing up, my parents were a bit feisty with each other. Dad was from Brooklyn and mom was from Mobile, and the fireworks in the home could be incredible. Often, my sister, Debbie, and I would go to our rooms, sometimes in tears.

"If God didn't believe we could handle this, we would never have been made preacher's kids," she would say.

Sometimes, as I walk through life with a limp because of a scar on my heart, I am grateful that God walks with me. Together, we can handle whatever comes next.

WHO SAID YOU WEREN'T PERFECT?

Melanie and her husband have been attending Metro Life Church for many years, since we were first planted. Their son, Benjamin, was the first child I dedicated.

God is right there with you. He doesn't allow something to happen to you that you and He can't bear together.

Their second son, Nicholas, was only six months old when Melanie showed up at Mary's office with a sheet of paper in hand, tears streaming down her face.

Unlike their first child, Melanie had noticed her son wasn't developing the same, and the delays had concerned her. At first, doctors told her to stop comparing Nicholas to her first child and that each child was unique. But the developmental delays continued and finally, a geneticist was able to tell them what was going on. He had a chromosomal disorder, chromosome 8p duplication deletion. This was very rare, with only five known cases at the time.

"I don't even know how to pray," she told Mary as she sat down, still clutching the piece of paper detailing the diagnosis, a piece of paper that told of physical and intellectual disability that seemed to be the end for the dreams they had for their family. The doctor had told her that their son would have severe cognitive and physical disabilities. Internal organs would be at risk for failure. Their lives would be changed from that moment on.

"Melanie, that paper is not going to define your son," Mary told her, and they began to pray.

Melanie was mad at God; maybe that's why it was hard to pray. She was a good Christian. She served at church, read her Bible, did all the right things. This wasn't fair.

"Why me, God?"

Yet even as she wrestled with God, He was patient and was at work. She remembered how after Nicholas went through yet another brain scan, the neurologist again told her all of the things that might happen to her son, but then surprised her with his words.

"Those things might happen, yes," he said, "but you're going to raise him as if they're not going to. You'll treat him as if nothing is wrong with him. He's going to experience life. You'll teach him math. You'll laugh at his jokes."

As Nicholas grew older and regular visits to specialists and therapists became the norm, Melanie began to see God's blessings. She watched as he surpassed expectations, learning to speak. His first word, at age four, was *mom*. He was a super happy, joyful kid. When he comes into a room, it lights up. His smile was pure joy, and he's an important presence at the church.

Nicholas is in his twenties now, though intellectually much younger. He lives at home with his parents. He goes to an adult day care during the day, and he also has a volunteer job at a horse farm. He can talk, and he absolutely loves life. He doesn't have any of the physical health challenges that were part of that diagnosis. Unlike most people with chromosome 8p duplication deletion, many of whom are much more incapacitated than he is, he doesn't have seizures.

Nicholas has challenges, yes, but he's exceeded the prognosis and he has great abilities.

On the other side of wrestling with God, Melanie saw the work He was doing. It was her son's situation that brought her husband back to church, and Melanie was transformed herself.

"Don't you all get tired of praying for the same thing?" she said to a friend when asked to pray for his wife, who had a chronic illness. It was early on, shortly after Nicholas's diagnosis, and she told him how every day she prayed for his healing, that he would be perfect.

"Who told you he wasn't perfect, Melanie?" the friend asked.

That was the moment she went from praying in beggar mode to gratitude mode, loving and appreciating God. She was able to be thankful for her husband and both her sons and a great life. Once she shifted from constantly staring at the pain, it set her on fire and she began writing about her journey, ministering to parents with disabled kids.

People come up to her now and notice her joy. "You're really happy," they tell her and her husband. "You do better than I do with my 'normal' kids."

Nicholas's life introduces people to God in a non-threatening and unique way. Melanie and her husband, in the same way, inspired me after my heart attack.

If they can make it through, so can I, I remember thinking.

It's 2 Corinthians 1:3–4 in action, where our endlessly compassionate God gives us comfort so that we can provide comfort to others in the same way. He turns our pain into something incredibly beautiful for those who are hurting around us.

Maybe you lost heart and faith and took to the sidelines because of your limp. Maybe you're trying to limp through life right now, and you're discouraged by your slow pace. Maybe you're comparing yourself to others and can't help but feel less than perfect.

I don't know your situation, but I know what it's like to feel like a broken jar of clay that can't be used again. Your limp is the doorway for God to use you for His glory, if you'll let Him.

Because who told you that you weren't perfect for the plan He intended, limp and all?

Chapter Six

The Wall

"Good fences make for good neighbors," the man said to his neighbor as they met at the property line to fix the broken rock wall that separated their properties. Mending the wall was part of the arrival of spring, and the sunny day with its light breeze seemed made for working outside.

The neighbor was less convinced. "What if we just let the wall fall down?" he asked, his eyes running up and down the length of the structure, noting a few signs of collapse in progress with wayward stones pulled down by gravity.

"We've always had a wall here," the man said, pulling on his work gloves. It would take a few hours to get all of the stones back into place.

"What is the wall for?" the neighbor asked, watching the man begin to struggle with the heavy stones. "What are we trying to keep out?"

The man sighed, and, setting the rock down, stood up to meet the neighbor's eyes. "This is what we do. We build walls. We've always kept this wall here. It's what we've always done."

There might be nothing to wall in or out, but the main thing is that the wall had to stay.

This is the story of Robert Frost's "Mending Walls," a poem about two neighbors who regularly fix the rock wall between their property. One insists on the wall, while the other isn't so sure. The point Frost is making is worth considering, when it comes to walls we build in our life. Why are they there? Why do we maintain them or keep them up? Do we realize we're doing it?

"I've hit a wall," is a phrase we hear from athletes or creatives—anyone trying to accomplish something—who has suddenly lost their direction or motivation. They're stuck where they're at, but at least they realize they're at the wall.

When confronted with a wall in life, too many of us don't realize what's in front of us. It would be nice if we could march around it and defeat it with trumpets and shouts, like Joshua and the Israelites, but we would have to be aware of its existence first.

So the wall stays.

We stop moving. Our dreams fade away. We set up camp and accept that we'll live our lives there, in the shadow of the wall.

I don't know what your wall is, whether it's an inability to look past yourself, or your own fears, or your personal history. What I do know is that you don't have to stay there. You can get past it to the other side, a place where you can dream again. But first you need to understand what you're up against. You need to be able to spot the wall.

*When confronted with
a wall in life, too many
of us don't realize
what's in front of us.*

TRAUMA CREATES WALLS

I wouldn't consider myself an aggressively ambitious guy, not in the way most people would think of it. I have always been motivated by results. I liked growth and progress. I was never the person busy building my own kingdom. I didn't see myself as a driver.

After the heart attack, I was "lunch pail" guy, all about getting to the work site, getting the work done, making sure it was done right, and then going home. Because I was in survival mode, I was just happy to be there and be present. I wasn't focused on what I was missing, but instead, how I was feeling.

"What am I missing out on?" was replaced by "how will I get through today?"

My doctor had told me that any pain I felt from the waist up was going to cause me fear and anxiety, and he was right. Gas or indigestion made me wonder if the Big One was coming. When something traumatic happens to you, a wall goes up. It's a defensive wall that is reasonable at first because it helps protect you, but eventually that wall becomes rooted in fear and impossible to move past.

I was checking off each day, literally shutting down thoughts and plans for tomorrow by focusing on clocking through the current day. I survived the week just so I could get to Sunday. When I got to Sunday, everything was fine; and so I'd do it again the coming week.

Life was a twenty-four-hour cycle to get to Sunday because Sunday was a kind of support system filled with people who loved and cared and checked in on how I was feeling. There was some good in that, in the early days. Sunday kind of became a test of how the week went, how I felt, what I accomplished, what habits and lifestyle changes were taking root.

This is why I said earlier that I could barely preach to the people because I was preaching to myself even more. It's as if someone hit a pause button on the movie of my life and halted any advancement whatsoever. Church growth wasn't my measure of success. Forward motion wasn't my measure of success. Building towards my dreams wasn't my measure of success. Survival of each day was my *only* measure of success.

SURVIVAL OF EACH DAY WAS MY *ONLY* MEASURE OF SUCCESS.

Initially that measure of success was fine. I had to reduce stress and heal from the heart attack. It's fine to run in survival mode early on, but it can't be forever. Yet trauma drops a wall in front of you and makes it so easy to forget that. If you never hit the play button again, that movie sits on pause forever.

MISTAKING HOLDING PATTERNS FOR FORWARD MOVEMENT

It's winter and you're one of the frozen chosen from up north, longing for the sunny, warm beaches of Florida and the vacation you've been planning for months.

After three hours of flight, you're looking forward to arriving at your destination. You're all packed for a week at the beach, sitting in the tiny airline seat with your legs cramping and your knees banging up against the seat in front of you. As your seat-mate jabs you in the side with his elbow yet again, you realize you'd take a walk down Any Street, USA just to stretch your legs right now, beach or not. Anything to get off of this airplane.

You can feel the airplane descending, and the seat belt light pops on with that familiar ding. The screen in front of you shows a giant airplane icon hovering over your destination and you know it's going to be mere moments before your vacation starts.

"Folks, weather near the airport has caused some backup in the skies," the pilot's voice says over the intercom. "We're going to be in a holding pattern for about twenty or thirty minutes until it's our turn to land. Thank you for your patience."

The sound of a collective groan goes up from the passengers.

You're surprised because you'd been on the plane so long, moving towards your destination, that you didn't realize the movement had shifted. If the pilot hadn't announced it, you might not have realized the change until a lot of time had passed. But even in the holding pattern, the airplane is still moving. The destination is in sight. Surely this is progress, right?

It really isn't. Never mistake a holding pattern for forward movement.

After the heart attack, even while in survival mode, I thought I was handling life pretty well. We started traveling a little bit. We went up to the condo in Stuart and began socializing with family and friends like we had before. The kids were doing well. I was back preaching at church. We were busy. It didn't feel like my life was missing anything because we were doing things. A busy life is a life of progress, right?

I didn't realize I was in a holding pattern. All the activities of daily life had distracted me from the reality that I wasn't actually going anywhere. Like a rubber ball, I was still pinging off of the wall in front of me. There's plenty of room to move around behind it; and for too many people, that's as far as they get. A comfortable, busy life after surviving something traumatic seems like a win, doesn't it?

God had placed a calling on my life, and while the heart attack and everything that came with it seemed to interrupt things significantly, the calling was still there. Yet embracing survival mode seemed to neutralize my calling. Rising up to meet the call of God in your life requires forward motion. It requires getting past walls and looking to the future.

 NEVER MISTAKE A HOLDING PATTERN FOR FORWARD MOVEMENT.

Looking back at that time is actually scary because I can see how easy it would have been to think I was going places when I wasn't. I could have stayed where I was and still be there to this day. You have to be able to see the wall to move past it, and for the longest time, I didn't. I let it limit my thinking.

Before the heart attack, I looked at life through a window. Through it, I could see out in the distance, surveying everything before me and partnering with God on how to improve or make change to what was ahead. This was about building the Body of Christ.

All I could see was myself and my life and my fears and what I was comfortable doing.

After the heart attack, I looked at life in a mirror. The window was gone, and I had no outward view. All I could see was myself and my life and my fears and what I was comfortable doing.

Self-focus is a strange beast. Your vision becomes nearsighted instead of farsighted; plans for the future fall off the radar. Self-focus can make you self-conscious to the degree that you become trapped in worry about what others think of you and what you're doing. That makes it easier to stick to what people think is normal or acceptable behavior instead of taking risks.[9]

"My doctor said to avoid stress, so that's what I'm doing," I would tell people when they asked how I was doing. And while that was true at the beginning, how long was I going to use that reasoning when it came to growing the church? Inevitably, people would nod and agree, and sitting in that holding pattern felt like the wise thing to do.

Self-focus also leads to ruminating about yourself or your past over and over and over, going so deep down the hole that even the mere suggestion that you ought to look outward instead of inward is unbelievably shocking.

When a wall pops up in front of a window, you notice. When a wall pops up in front of the mirror, you don't.

Often, it's about timing. Survival mode will help you get off a sinking ship. A holding pattern is fine if there's no room to land right now and you're waiting for bad weather to pass by.

---

[9] "Can You Be Too Self-Aware?" *Psychology Today*, Sussex Publishers, https://www.psychologytoday.com/us/blog/the-clarity/201909/can-you-be-too-self-aware.

But eventually the adrenaline crashes and the fuel tank runs dry and you must confront the wall.

TAKE BACK WHAT WAS STOLEN

We know people who have stayed at the wall after a crisis or trauma for a long, long time. And maybe if I was more ambitious before the heart attack, I would have been more depressed during this time, frustrated that I wasn't building my great empire. In fact, because I felt that I had my priorities in place before the heart attack, that I wasn't overly aggressive with people and the church, that I wasn't fixated on power, the heart attack felt like punishment.

"God, was I abusive towards people? Did I neglect something in Your church? Did I neglect time with You?" I would pray.

The wall is symbolic of what is standing in your way that needs to come down, including that sense that it's all about you, and you're being punished because something bad happened.

A friend had a failure in marriage. His wall was forgiveness, getting to the place where he could finally say that he could forgive his wife. He was hurt so badly that he couldn't get there. He didn't realize that his wife's betrayal had caused a rift in his relationship with God because everything he was thinking had "I" in it.

"I'm hurt."

"I was betrayed."

"I was humiliated."

"I didn't deserve this."

"I had my feelings hurt."

One of the ways you might realize you're at a wall is that your thinking is full of "I" and "me." I could see that in my friend.

"It's not wrong to process this kind of stuff at the beginning," I told him. "But I promise you that one day, if you can get past it, you'll look around and you'll start thinking in terms of "we" again."

I knew this was important for him to understand, or he'd do something foolish.

"Don't make a decision right now to leave or get a divorce," I said. "Don't tell everyone all of the things you're telling me in private. Don't feed the anger in others to justify what you feel. Process, but fight hard."

You'll start seeing the future, and the wall in front of it, when you start seeing outside of yourself. The enemy wants you to keep turning inward, but that's dangerous because he's stealing from you when he succeeds.

One night, during a time when Gaby was struggling with some health issues, she woke up around 4 a.m. while the rest of us were asleep. She looked out the front window of the house and saw that there was a light inside one of the cars in the driveway. At first she thought it was moonlight, but then she looked closer and realized it was a man in a hat holding a flashlight, breaking into our cars.

"Hey, get out of our car!" she yelled, pounding on the window and making all kinds of noise. I woke up quickly and ran for the door in my bare feet. I leaped across the front sidewalk towards the driveway, hurtling for the car. The man was clearly surprised but managed to get out of the car and run away. We called the police, but they weren't able to find him.

We all felt violated. We were groggy and had been ripped out of our sleep by panic and adrenaline. We'd seen the guy who had gone through our vehicles, and he was still out there. I could tell my family was nervous and upset.

"Guys, we're not going to go to sleep until we can laugh about this," I said. "I know it was scary, but we need to confront this now. We're not going to bed until we get our peace back."

Chris spoke up, tentatively at first, and told of how he'd jumped out of bed to save the day for his family, only to have his stocking feet betray him and send him tumbling to the floor. There were a few snickers.

"Wow, good job Chris."

The mood began shifting.

We joked a bit about Gaby, and the "special words" she used when she hollered at the thief. She pointed out my impressive feat of parkour.

"I saw you jump across the driveway. What were you going to do if you caught him?"

Soon we were all laughing.

That thief was trying to take things out of our cars, but more than our possessions, he'd robbed us of our peace. And we had to take it back.

When a heart attack happens, when a spouse cheats, when a thief comes to steal, you have a decision to make. The wall falls down when you decide to be on the other side of it and take back what was stolen.

One afternoon, Mary and I were sitting together in the church. There were no lightning bolts or earthquakes, just me with my arm around Mary, leaning back and chatting. A wall

The wall falls down when
you decide to be
on the other side of it
and take back what
was stolen.

caught my eye. I started to look around and an idea began to grow.

"This building is too small," I said to her. "We have to take that wall down."

That was the moment I started looking through a window again instead of in a mirror. I didn't want to live in survival mode anymore, apparently, but wanted to see the church grow. Even if my family and friends had wanted to move forward, it was me that had a finger on that pause button. And now I was pressing play.

It's the person who has had the tragedy, the setback, the trauma who controls what happens with the wall. As much as those who love you might want you to move on, they can't bring down that wall for you.

At some point, you have to give yourself permission to go back to normal, to let the enemy know he's taken everything from you he's going to get. You have to give yourself permission to overcome the shame of your past, and the fear and worry about tomorrow. You need to surrender to the process of healing because it's going to push you right against the wall and make you see it for what it is.

Are you maintaining a wall that shouldn't be there? Are you in a holding pattern and mistaking it for movement? If so, that wall has kept you for long enough from seeing how much bigger and better your life could be. It's skewed your perspective and kept you from seeing a brighter life on the other side.

Now is the time to move past it. Now is the time to reawaken the dreamer in you.

Chapter Seven

Reawakening
The Dreamer

The dreamer in you just needs a punch in the face. Hear me out on this one.

Once we decided to remove a wall to open the space in the church, we calculated that we needed one and a half million dollars to make it happen. When we first got the building, years before my heart attack, we'd tried to do some necessary remodeling that cost about half of that, but raising the funds was a struggle and we couldn't seem to move the needle.

Ten years later, after my heart attack, there we were, needing another remodel but with a bigger price tag. Memories of the struggle to raise the funds filled me with dread.

I remember the first evening we took the leap, during a praise and worship service. I made the announcement about needing to raise money to remove the wall. As I stepped down off of the platform and moved to the back of the room, people began rushing to the front to put their giving commitments on the platform. I was taken by surprise.

"This time it's going to be easy," God seemed to tell me. "This time you won't be up front at the pulpit, pulling them across the finish line, you'll be behind them, only needing to give encouragement."

At that moment, I was literally seeing what God was telling me would happen *as* it happened. I was behind the people and they were streaming up to the platform and I don't think anything could have stopped them. He was right. It was the easiest thing we ever did financially. There was no criticism, no pushback. The money was raised very quickly.

"THIS TIME IT'S GOING TO BE EASY," GOD SEEMED TO TELL ME.

The first time we'd tried to raise money, before the heart attack, it almost killed me. We couldn't remove the literal church wall because there was some kind of spiritual wall that was holding people back. This time was different. Their love for the church and for the need and for me and my family was almost tangible.

The success and positive experience of that project helped the church grow even more and seemed to open doors to what we needed to do next. The following project involved much more serious remodeling, moving the platform to a different side to maximize the space. We also wanted to add more classrooms and other space like a store and studio for the worship team. The church was growing rapidly, and we knew we had to make better use of the space to accommodate the growth.

When I went over the costs with some of the guys from church who were helping with the construction, one asked why it was going to cost so much. I explained that the music studio and the lights, along with other soft costs, added up. That's when one of my friends in the group spoke up.

"Wait a minute," he said. "Are you doing this for your wife? For your ego?"

There are several ways to know when you're no longer in a holding pattern, when you've moved beyond simply trying to survive, when you're awake inside and you have a big dream ready to explode out of you. I knew I'd fully embraced moving past the wall and towards the future because, in that moment, something stirred in me.

As it turns out, it was my fist.

I punched my friend straight in the face.

"Don't you ever accuse me of being egotistical and doing this for anything but the Kingdom," I said, shaking my hand while he massaged his cheek and regained his footing.

He and I were good friends (still are), like brothers even, but that was a moment. I might not have been an ambitious guy, but I was an aggressive guy in some situations. There's a reason I liked Ray "Boom Boom" Mancini. And while my aggression has toned down since then, it was a significant shift from three years of fear-based survival to fighting for the future by taking a swing at my friend's face.

I don't advise you to take a swing at your friend's face. I do advise you to reawaken the dreamer and feel that fight for the future inside of you.

MOVING FORWARD, DESPITE
BAD HARVESTS

Remember how I told you about sowing and reaping a bad harvest? This plays into whether you move beyond the wall or stay stuck.

First, remember that there are two kinds of harvests, the one you sowed for, and the one you didn't. Sometimes bad things happen, like being fired from your job or losing your home to a fire, even though you never sowed for it.

When you order something online and the wrong product comes, you send it back. In the same way, when you get a harvest for something you didn't sow for, you send it back. You refuse to receive it. You don't pull it inside and make it your identity; instead, you walk in the direction of a better harvest. Even if you've made mistakes along the way, you can still choose which direction you'll walk in.

We had a heart for helping pregnant young women who had no support system or options for help. Several years before my heart attack, we decided to take a giant step and support a ministry to help those young women. We bought a beautiful home on a gorgeous rural lot in the Redlands. Mango groves, rolling green pasture—it was literally a place of peace, and we invested large amounts of money into making it work. We brought on staff, set up guidelines, and prepared to take in young women in need of help. We had a van to transport the children and located a daycare for the babies, as the girls went to school. We tried to connect with businesses to help sponsor what we were doing but couldn't find any private funds. Public funds were directed towards education, not a program like this. The financial squeeze quickly multiplied.

The ministry never manifested. The finances never balanced out, and we ended up taking out a line of credit on the facility. At one point, we had three young women in the program, but they had struggles that we hadn't anticipated. After two years of trying, we gave it one more year before pulling up stakes.

The third year was not the charm. We ended up selling the building and going into debt about a hundred thousand dollars. I felt like it was a failure on my part that we couldn't get that ministry up and running. And even though we honored our commitment to pay off the debt and didn't tarnish our relationship or reputation in the community, I consider it one of the biggest mistakes of my leadership. It was a bad harvest.

I thought that was the dream.

I thought that was what a person in my position should be doing.

I thought we should have more skin in the game and give the project a real shot.

We got a bad harvest anyway.

It's strange how a dream—and the noisy and embarrassing crashing of it—can create a wall that stops you from dreaming again. Bad harvests and walls have the same problem: how do you go forward?

We could've stayed there, throwing more money at the failure, reneging on our debts, or pointing the finger somewhere else. We could've held the line at the wall. But the only way out of a bad harvest, the only way past the wall, is to sow new and better seed.

Bad harvests and walls have the same problem: how do you go forward?

In 2 Samuel 12, we watch King David sow and reap a bad harvest in record time. He lusts after another man's wife (Bathsheba), gets her pregnant, tries to hide it, and ultimately has the husband killed in battle. David and Bathsheba's child dies soon after birth. That was his harvest.

It's a story that almost exceeds belief, particularly because King David was a man after God's own heart. How could he, of all people, plant those seeds? And how do you get past that wall of shame and guilt and grief now in front of you?

In David we see how it's done because the first thing he does is go to God and repent. You can't repent a harvest you didn't sow, but David had most certainly sowed incredible evil. Part of that repentance is recognizing what caused the bad harvest. God is called the Lord of the Harvest, which means He is still in control. I must change the seed I'm planting. I can't blame a bad harvest on God that came from my seed.

After that, you have to ride out the bad harvest. You can't shorten its duration; time will have to pass, and the season will have to come to completion. What happens when the harvest is over?

As long as you're making sure to sow good seeds, it will be much better.

Good seed, like asking for forgiveness from people we've hurt, like making changes in our life to be more healthy, like returning what we've stolen, like walking in righteous principles. Haggai 2:9 tells us that the other side of that bad harvest, the other side of that wall, can be greater than the former. That's why, even while riding out a bad harvest, there's room for hope and joy.

God made us to think eternally, and that's why the enemy loves to see you stuck behind a wall, looking in a mirror. He wants you to keep that bad harvest in view, always lurking behind you. He wants you to forget that a new season is always coming and with it, the hope of a new and better harvest.

YOUR HEART WILL BEAT AGAIN

It was the summer of 1997. I was thirty-seven years old, and I had just resigned from Grace Church to go start Metro Life Church. I'd made a promise to my dad to go to a Promise Keepers event with the men from Grace Church, but after that, I was officially done there. It was the messy end of a very difficult season in our lives, where strife and drama were constant every Sunday; and I was weary of it all.

The morning of the event, Mary came to me.

"Steve, I feel sick."

"I can stay home with you," I told her. I hated to see her sick. I'd rather be with her than at the event, anyway.

"No, you go ahead and do what you have to do," she said, wanting me to honor my commitment.

During the Promise Keepers event, I couldn't get her out of my mind, so during a break I went downstairs at the arena and found a payphone.

"Mary, are you okay?" I asked her when she picked up the phone.

"Steve, I'm pregnant!" Mary answered.

Our first two children had been born out of a struggle with infertility; we'd had to go to specialist after specialist to conceive. My family's struggles were almost a mirror of what was happening at the church, with our dream to birth a new church full of hardship.

I was ecstatic at Mary's news, and I can tell you that I don't remember much else about that day, besides hearing those words. Lauren was the first child in our family who came without the trial. In a way, she represented a new season in our lives. We couldn't have seen it coming, but maybe we should have.

Early one morning during a hunting trip a few years ago, as Mary and I watched the sun come up, she told me about "the dawn chorus." Near sunrise, birds often sing more loudly and vigorously than they do at other times of the day. It's as if they're instinctively responding to the rising sun, greeting the new day with excitement and expectation. Do you know who appreciates sunrise more than anyone? Someone coming out of a bad night.

> WHEN IT'S YOUR DARKEST HOUR,
> IT'S HARD TO BELIEVE LIGHT
> WILL EVER SHINE AGAIN.

The day after my heart attack, I couldn't wait for the sun to rise. I'd had the worst night of my life, and I needed to see those rays of warm light come in through the hospital windows. When things are dark, you're not sure if you have a future, you're in a holding pattern thinking only about surviving, dwelling on all the what-ifs. And then the sun comes up.

When it's your darkest hour, it's hard to believe light will ever shine again. When the harvest is so bad, it's hard to believe a new season will come your way. When you're stopped at the wall, it's hard to believe you'll ever move forward. When your heart is broken, it's hard to believe it'll ever work the same.

CCM artists Phillips, Craig and Dean wrote "Tell Your Heart To Beat Again," a song based on an incredible true story. According to them, a surgeon finished open heart surgery on a woman, and everything went well. He massaged the heart to get it to pump on its own, but it did not. The surgeon tried again. The heart didn't move. The surgical team tried a few more extreme measures to get the heart to pump, but nothing worked. Finally, the surgeon knelt down beside the table, pulled down his surgical mask, and spoke gently into the unconscious patient's ear.

"The surgery went perfectly," he said. "Your heart is fine now. Tell your heart to beat again."

At that moment, the heart twitched and began to pump.

The heart is capable, but you have to believe. God is at work on your heart, and He's trying to tell you that your heart can beat again. Difficult things happen in life, sometimes of our making and sometimes not. The world is full of people stalled in that moment, people who aren't sowing something better, or who have decided to build a shelter next to the wall and stay put. They think in terms of surviving, not fully reviving. They devote so much time to worry and fear that they can't find time to dream of the future.

But not you.

You can live again.

You can have life, and *more* abundantly.

If you can believe that, then you are ready to finish well.

Chapter Eight

Finishing Well

Don Shula is a true legend.

First a defensive back and then a coach in the National Football League, Shula spent most of his career coaching my hometown team, the Miami Dolphins. He took us Floridians through the greatest season in football history: an undefeated, Super Bowl winning year in 1972 that defied all odds when his star quarterback, Bob Griese, was injured after only five games and had to be replaced by thirty-eight-year-old Earl Morrall.

Mom loved football, and our whole family went to every home game. Every Sunday, church would start at 11 a.m. and Dad would finish preaching the service just in time for us to hit the road, grab something to eat at Burger King, and walk into the stadium on time to see Garo Yepremian kick the ball for the game to get under way. The Miami Dolphins, and Shula, own some important real estate in my childhood memory.

Shula coached for thirty-three years and is the winningest coach in NFL history.

But it's not just his victories that make him a legend. He led championship teams and had endless opportunities before him, with every right to grab hold of fame and celebrity (with all its perks). Instead, he chose to stay in his community and give back to it, putting value on family and values instead of relishing wealth and fame.

A few years ago, I was fortunate enough to meet Don Shula. I was at a country club having dinner with my family when we heard a general rumble from the people there. We started looking around to see who had arrived, and that's when we saw him. He wasn't a physically imposing figure, but he seemed larger than life because of his career and what he'd accomplished. I took a chance and walked over to introduce myself and tell how much I admired his career and life. And do you know what Shula did? He returned my handshake with a firm grip and a broad smile, never once acting like he was above me or didn't have time for me, and my respect for him grew even more.

On the way out of his career, Shula didn't win as many games as he once had; but he was still determined to finish well. His career was a success because of more than the wins he collected. He was respected by his team, by his family, and by just about anyone who ever met him. You couldn't look back on his career or his life outside of football and point a finger at any scandal or black mark.

Don Shula finished well.

We live in a world that fixates on the starting gate and on who's ahead or behind. When we're consumed with the need for flashy speed, we're setting ourselves up for failure. We can't finish well if we don't finish our race at all.

"I've fought the good fight," Paul wrote in 2 Timothy 4:7–8.

But he had something more to say. "I have *finished* the race and I have kept the faith."

Paul started off as a powerful Roman citizen, a persecutor of Christians. He ended up imprisoned and eventually put to death. But he kept his sights on finishing well, and that's what we need to do, too. We can get caught up with what happened at the starting gate or what's going on during the race and feel discouraged when setbacks cause us to fall behind. But none of that matters as long as you remember it's about fighting the good fight and keeping the faith.

It's all about how you finish.

> ## WE CAN'T FINISH WELL IF WE DON'T FINISH OUR RACE AT ALL.

FORGET THE STARTING GATE

Some wondered if it was even possible. Not since Citation in 1948 had any horse won the Triple Crown. To win the three required races—the Kentucky Derby, the Preakness Stakes, and the Belmont Stakes—was no easy feat. They were strenuous races that happened over a short span of time and required a spectacular horse.

And then came 1973, and Secretariat.

Secretariat had recently come in third place at the Wood Memorial, beaten by Sham, the Derby favorite, and one other. There was doubt about how Secretariat would do at his next race, the Kentucky Derby. Sham was a fast horse, and when the starting bell rang at the Kentucky Derby, he came out of the starting gate quickly and stayed at the front of the pack. Secretariat, on the other hand, seemed to emerge from the gate as an afterthought in comparison, hovering around the back making sure his jockey, Ron Turcotte, ate dirt for most of the race.

But then, as the other horses felt the long track eating up their energy, Secretariat pounded up the stretch from behind. Instead of cutting in and hugging the rail where the distance was shorter, he roared by on the outside, crossing the finish line a few lengths ahead of Sham. The same thing happened at the Preakness Stakes. As it turned out, given enough track, Secretariat showed he could finish well.

The final race, the Belmont Stakes, was the longest of the three. By now the race had the attention of a nation that had waited almost thirty years for a Triple Crown winner. Everyone had an opinion on what would happen, on which horse would win and how they should do it.

When the starting bell rang and the gates were flung open, both horses leapt to the front almost stride-for-stride. Fast Sham, no stranger to the front, quickly set a grueling pace and both horses pulled away from the rest of the pack. But this time, Secretariat stayed with him. Somewhere around the backstretch, an exhausted Sham fell back while Secretariat actually *gained* speed as he neared the finish, eventually winning the race by thirty-one lengths and setting track records that have yet to be broken to this day.

What happens at the starting bell and during the race matters less than what happens at the finish line.

Now that's a great story of success; but it's also a story about a hard run, one where you feel like you're losing, you learn from it, and you keep going. We love the story of a long shot, of someone who comes from behind for the win, or of someone who surprises everyone and pulls off an unimaginable victory. We love those stories, except when they are in our own lives. Being the long shot and at the back of the pack is disheartening when you're there. That kind of race feels like failure for most of the run, in the shadow of the frontrunners, eating their dirt. Giving up looks like the smart choice.

But the finish line is still calling you.

What happens at the starting bell and during the race matters less than what happens at the finish line. Everything we've done in our race of life will show itself there. Will you blame others for your losses? Will you cheat to get ahead? Will you wear yourself out trying to be in front from the start? Will you keep going to the finish line? Will you see the victory in finishing, no matter who is ahead of you?

Think about those stickers you see on the back of cars, the black and white circles with 26.2 emblazoned on them. You don't see what place that person came in when they ran that marathon. All you see is that they finished, that they ran the full course. The message is clear: when the race itself is the battle, the act of finishing is the victory. Whether you're first or 100th.

It's easy enough to leap out of the gates to the front, setting a fast and impressive pace, but few can keep that pace to the end. Maybe you've racked up some failures in life. But how you've run in the past doesn't define how you will run in the future, and it doesn't have to define how you will cross that finish line.

In a race, the person who knows themselves, and their physical and emotional limitations, can find the rhythm of the run. They are able to create a strategy without getting overwhelmed by what's happening at the moment. They are unswayed by the noisy fans cheering or booing, nor are they dismayed by their place in the pack. They are the real contender. They might not run the flashiest race, but they can stay on pace until the end. That's the person who, when others falter, can keep going. And their win is all the more victorious because they didn't quit no matter how impossible the race seemed at the start.

If you feel like you're so far behind that it's too late for you, that a destroyed marriage or a bankruptcy or a massive heart attack has taken you out of the running, I want to assure you that you're still in the race. It's still possible to cross that finish line with your head held high. At this very moment, you have a future where you can finish well.

YOU CAN'T BE CONSISTENT IF YOU LIVE COMPARATIVELY

The art of finishing well is rooted in godly consistency. Distractions have no place in the plan. You have to keep going forward in a way that is honoring God. The world has lots of distractions to offer you, especially in the form of comparison to others. The world is all too happy to see you lose focus on the finish line God has set for you and to look elsewhere.

I joke that being one of the few who survived a heart attack that kills nearly 90 percent of people is the only time I've been at the top of any list. But in a way, it's true. I was a late bloomer, and that meant I developed a bit slower and seemed to be behind the curve—never ahead—in just about everything. Once I learned something, though, it was a different story. I could grab on and stick with it.

In high school, I had a friend named Tito, a dark-haired guy with blue eyes. We called ourselves Starsky and Hutch; I was Starsky, and Tito was Hutch. The girls really liked Tito.

"I know you're here for Tito's blue eyes," I'd joke with the girls, "but stick around and you'll like me better in the long run."

Given enough time, I could wear down the opposition. Given enough of a racetrack, I could finish well. I've learned it's important to understand that no matter what it seems like right now, there's opportunity ahead of you. By the time you get closer to the finish line, things can be better.

Unless, of course, you've surrounded yourself with the wrong people or even good people who don't bring out the best in you. I can't emphasize enough how important it is to choose carefully who you do the journey of life with and how hard you have to work to silence the voices of comparison in your own head.

Imagine you and your friends decide to do a 5K "fun" run. You're not really a serious runner, but you can complete the three miles given enough time. One of your friends, however, goes for a run every morning. When the race starts, his pace is much faster than yours. What he sees as just encouraging you to go faster is actually going to wear you out and keep you from finishing at all. You'll become discouraged, and all you'll get from the run is a comparison between your supposed lack of speed and your friend's quickness and fitness level.

Good friend, good runner, but not the best one to partner for that run.

A few years after my heart attack, some of the church staff, along with Mary and I, actually did enter a 5K. People wanted to encourage me in my health journey, and while we all ran the race, our paces weren't the same. And that was okay. Some ran it entirely, while others slowed down and walked across the finish line. But the point is that we all finished. We just had to go at our own pace to do it.

All around us are people running at different paces, and it's tempting to compare yourself to what they're doing. Maybe you increase your pace in an attempt to keep up and act like something you're not, wearing yourself out long before the finish line because you tried to just stick with the crowd. The people you're surrounded by might be above you or below you. They might be in front of you or behind you. But it's the ones running next to you that are the most important.

For me, choosing who I'll run next to starts with first impressions. That sounds odd, but I think the Lord allows me to see a person clearly early on. I see how they live their life, what's going on in their family. Do their kids like them as well as love them? What's their relationship with their spouse? Their friends? How do they behave around other people? Do they flock to the important people, or are they like Don Shula, genuine enough to shake hands with an average guy no matter their status?

In Hebrews 12:1–2, we're reminded that we're surrounded by a great cloud of witnesses. And because of that, we ought to throw off any sin that is entangling us and causing us to stumble on the track. We are to run with perseverance, using the heart God put in us for the unique race God marked for us.

If you're running with a crowd that's trying to lay their heart's desire and their race on you, you won't finish well. They might be great people and have great intentions, but they're going to trip you up. You weren't intended to run their race at their pace. You weren't intended to rely on them so much that you think you need those people beside you, and you end up comparing yourself to them at every step.

My first mentor was a well-known man in the world of business. Early on, I *needed* his help. But over time, that changed to simply *wanting* his guidance. That is, I was able to move from thinking I needed to run stride-for-stride next to him to began running my own race instead using the advice and tips he gave me.

THE DISTRACTION OF COMPARING YOURSELF TO OTHERS CAN SEND YOU DOWN THE WRONG PATH.

After the heart attack, I discovered that I didn't need outside validation of the way I was running my race, even though many of the people I *needed* early on I still enjoyed having around. Realizing that was transforming.

The distraction of comparing yourself to others can send you down the wrong path. The people you surround yourself with, whether it's your friends or teachers you're listening to, will determine if you'll be consistent or distracted. Consistency gets you to the finish line, while comparison does the opposite.

THE ART OF FINISHING WELL

HBO's 2019 documentary *Belichick and Saban: The Art of Coaching* gave viewers an inside look at how two of the most successful NFL and college coaches kept a forty-year friendship alive, mixed in with their coaching philosophies.

After each season, Belichick and Saban would get together and go over the season, debriefing each other on what happened. It was a classic case of iron sharpening iron. Both coaches had one particular thing they'd say to the athletes: "Just do your job!"

You know why that was so successful? Because they could teach the players what their job was. A complex game, broken down into specific jobs, is doable. Do your job and stop worrying about everyone else's.

The problem is that too many people want to be taught, but not enough want to learn. Being taught is a passive act. Learning is the action. We are capable of learning what God has for us, for our race, because the Holy Spirit guides us in truth. While we need good pastors and teachers in our lives, God has enabled us to learn the principles specific to our unique race, the priorities we need to apply to our life no matter what stage we're at.

Finishing well might seem to be something people in the last half of their life have to worry about, but we forget that each race has different sections. A horse racing track has poles around it that measure furlongs, or an eighth of a mile. Car races might be gauged by which lap you're on. While running, the mile marker might be what you're paying attention to.

We are all in different seasons in our life, and each of those can be finished well. Whether you're twenty-five or eighty, finishing well matters wherever you are.

When I was in my twenties, I wasn't thinking about my golden years; just thinking about a five-year plan for anything was annoying.

"Hey, Steve, what's your five-year plan?"

"Stop bothering me. I'm trying to figure out this year's plan."

Getting through one year was hard enough, and the push to have a five-year plan felt like a motivational gimmick. I didn't have a five-year plan for my ministry, much less my life. I understand why a business that lives or dies on trends needs a long-term plan, but I'm not convinced you have to have a five-year plan to be a success in running your own personal race.

THE ART OF FINISHING WELL IS ABOUT ACTION.

Why?

Because consistency takes care of it all. Consistency in godly non-negotiable principles and understanding the concept of sowing and harvesting will take care of that. The only way to predict the future is by the seeds you sow today.

I take a micro view instead of a macro view. My behavior, my attitude, my thought life, the decisions I make—I have to flesh those out to honor God with every step. We see things happening in our own lives and our own society that clearly reveal too many aren't thinking this way. The seeds we're sowing as a culture will have a horrible harvest in ten years. By being passive and refusing to run a good race and fight the good fight, we're sowing seeds that we are possibly not even aware of.

The art of finishing well is about action. It's about consistently sticking to godly principles and surrounding yourself with the right people. Run the race God laid out for you and stop being distracted by everything happening around you because finishing well isn't just about you. It is a kind of domino effect, one that reaches in three directions: the generation before, the generation after, and right now.

Every day, when you head out the front door, there are two bags of seeds to choose from, good or bad. Which bag are you going to carry?

Conclusion:
Play The Long Game

Saul was great at his job, and because Christianity was growing across the Roman Empire, it seemed like job security as a young up-and-coming persecutor was solid. He was eager to root out those Christ-following heretics because, as both a Jewish Pharisee and a Roman citizen, everything they said and stood for was against what he considered good and right.

Even better than mere job security, Saul actually enjoyed his work. He found it fulfilling and was there to encourage others who were of the same mindset. That's why, when a young man named Stephen was thrown to the ground to be stoned to death for sharing the good news of Jesus Christ, Saul held the coats of those who'd do the stoning, so they could get on with it. His very breath was taken up with threatening the followers of Christ.

Saul had gotten permission from the high priests allowing him to go after any followers of Christ who were in the city of Damascus, so he booked his trip and hit the road with his crew. He had no idea what was about to happen.

We can be like Saul, so caught up in our busy work that we have no idea we might be on a completely wrong path. We take our cues from our apparent worldly success, thinking that all the applause from those around us must indicate we're doing what we should be doing. We have no idea how what we're doing may be pulling us away from what God wants.

Not all of us are as dramatically off the right path as Saul was, of course. But because God is loving, He can see our trajectory and will offer a course correction. Sometimes, that comes as a 42 moment.

As Saul and his entourage plodded down the road to Damascus, an intense light flashed from the sky. Saul fell to the ground, unable to do much once there.

"Saul, why are you persecuting me?" the voice of Jesus said, telling him who He was before giving Saul instructions to go to Damascus.

His entourage was a little freaked out. While they couldn't see the light, they could hear the sound. It didn't help that when Saul stood up, his open eyes couldn't see anything at all. He was at the mercy of his friends, who led him by the hand into Damascus. Not until Ananias, a follower of Christ who just days before would've been a target for Saul, prayed for him was he able to see.

You can read the whole story in Acts chapters 7 through 9, but maybe you know how it all worked out. Saul became Paul, one of the greatest evangelists of the early Christian church and a significant contributor to the New Testament before he was put to death. But he had to get knocked to the ground and learn to rely on faith in God to become who he was meant to be.

I know what it's like to get knocked to the ground. I wasn't persecuting Christians or anything of the sort, but for some reason God needed to get my attention and make a change in me through a heart attack.

"I have a different path for you," He seemed to say. "It's going to be a hard brake, but I'll be with you for the sharp turn."

42 moments aren't just singular events that make a blip on the radar. They are things that, when you look back, you realize they changed your life. I'm not just a guy who had a heart attack a few years ago. I'm a changed man because of that heart attack.

Your life doesn't become about the event. The event reminds you to be about life. Since those forty-two minutes of hovering near death, my commitment to the legacy I come from and the legacy I'm building has been validated.

Unlike Saul, my name wasn't changed. In fact, I love my last name. It's my family name, and I love what it represents: that New York Italian feel about the family, the masculine influence the name represents. There was a pioneer spirit, with my great-grandfather, Giovanni, coming from Italy to America to become a barber in Brooklyn. He later sent for his family to join him. My grandfather, Papa, was a good Catholic who became a welder in the Brooklyn Navy Yard. One day he was given a tract about Jesus, and he accepted Christ as his Savior. Ultimately, his entire household became saved, and

Since those forty-two minutes of hovering near death, my commitment to the legacy I come from and the legacy I'm building has been validated.

that led to the move to Florida. That spirit trickled down as my father and his brothers established churches in Miami.

I love that the legacy of a name can mean so much. But this is much more than being about a name because that name didn't keep my siblings or uncles or cousins in the faith. Some have left; some haven't finished well. There was immorality, even though the name and the legacy are still there. This is about the calling, and what my life as a whole will represent. That means we're playing the long game—and if you've gone through a 42 moment, that's the kind of game you're playing, too.

Put one foot in front of the other, sow good seed, and make the distance from the event to the future count. There is potential for abundance there. That has certainly proven true for my heart attack. If I can borrow from Charles Dickens' opening line in *A Tale of Two Cities* and adjust it a bit, it was the worst of times, and it was the best of times. That terrible moment was a major course correction, and I picked up a new bag of seeds to sow after that.

So how could I go back and say that 42 moment was a bad thing?

Since my 42, I've enjoyed so many wonderful blessings. Would I have recognized those blessings without it? Would they have come my way if my life hadn't been so radically changed that day?

I don't know.

What I do know is that the awful experience was actually a beautiful one from where I stand now. There are so many things I couldn't have done before that moment. I wouldn't have changed how I took care of my health. I wouldn't have completely grasped how precious life is. And I couldn't have written this book—a book about my life—one day sooner.

Please don't give up. Don't let your inability to understand the why behind the 42 stop you from planting good seeds for that future goal you have. That 42 is not the end, but the new beginning.

Like I said at the beginning of this book, when my 42 hit, I was down for the count. I was wondering if life was over. I was unsure how to get up off the mat. But I did. I picked myself up and continued the fight through those later rounds, even when the opponent seemed too big, too strong, too overwhelming. I was determined to finish well. I wrote this book based on the truth that if your heart's still beating, God's not finished with you.

Get up off the mat and keep fighting.

Later in life, Paul wrote that we are living testaments. If anyone would know, it would be him. We're a story in the making. Whatever 42 moment you've gone through or are going to go through, it isn't a mistake on the page but a turning point towards a new, abundant chapter.

My question for you, is what story will you write with your life?

Acknowledgements

I often tell the guys in my church that, when I pat them on the back or punch them on the arm or give an extra-long hug, it's worth 1000 words. I'm not much for long conversations. Once I get past the "how's it going?" or "what's going on?" or "family good?" I'm a bit lost and usually run out of things to say. But the following people believe all the pats, pinches, hugs, and words. Bear with me as I honor some very special people in my life that were there in 2007 when I was hit with my 42. People who have shaped who I am today.

To my wife, Mary, on October 10, 1987, our wedding day, we said words at the altar which became our vows for staying committed to our marriage. Words like "for better, for worse" and "in sickness and in health." Though they seemed like mere sayings in a ceremony, twenty years later you've shown me they were your heart. On June 17, 2007 *You! Chose! Life!* Wow...I sure needed you to do that for me when I couldn't do it for myself. Today, I'm grateful that each and every day

We! Choose! Love! Yes, I know I'm not the easiest person to love, but you do it. We have what we have today thanks in large part to you. You're easy and fun to love. Thank you for loving me more today and being the single greatest influence in my life. I love you!

To Christopher, Stephanie, Lolo and Gaby. It pretty much took a miracle to get each of you here, but once here, you've made something miraculous happen. You have made me a better man. My motivation to walk out what God has put in me was each of you, knowing you would be the first to see if I ever let my guard down. Now that I see the people you're each becoming, I'm inspired to reach even higher, love even deeper, fight even harder, and be even stronger. And you're keeping the challenge alive in me as you've brought Richelle, Muina, Gianna, and Marino into the family. Thank each of you for your love, honor, and commitment to the work your Mom and I have given our lives to and for running with the torch of Legacy. I love you!

To my sisters and in-laws on the Alessi side. There's an Italian saying "Il sangue non e acqua" which means "Blood is not water, so blood is thicker than water." Though our blood may sometimes reach the boiling point, when I needed you the most, you showed up. Thank you.

To Mary's side of the family, thank you for going to battle for your sister and me when our backs were against the wall. You know how to get in the ring and fight when the battle rages, and thankfully you've always been on the winning side. It's good to have you in my corner.

To my Uncle Paul Alessi and Aunt Wanda. Thank you for being the prayer warriors you are. All I remember as I laid in the emergency room was thinking, "I wish my Uncle Paul would come pray for me." I knew you to be a man of prayer.

To my dearest of friends, David and Mory Martinez, Manny and Laura Paula, and Tony and Angie Burke. I've always said that if a man can count just on one hand how many close friends he has, then he is blessed. My life is full because of your friendship. You were rocked when all hell broke loose in 2007, but you gathered yourselves and stayed committed to building what we started. Not once have you looked back in helping me build my life and my life's work. Others didn't stay on the journey, but you did. Thank you…for loving me, staying loyal to Mary and me, listening to all my sermons, remaining grounded, and giving it all as spotted sheep.

To our Metro Life Staff, Armando and Ana, Jonathon and Jackie, Desiree and Alton, Mory and David, Gianni and Angeline, Karina, Allen and Lia, Marcus and Ashley, and those who served back in 2007. The time spent together building the Kingdom is met with a promise. When we take care of God's people, He will take care of our people. There was no greater place to see that happen than when you stepped in to take care of Mary and me and our family. Thank you for your continued selflessness. Our work will be properly recognized when we all stand before God, and I pray we have prepared you in advance so you'll hear the words "well done thou good and faithful servants."

To our Metro Life Family, thank you for not allowing my stumble to cause you to lose a step in your faith pursuits. While I recovered you stayed true and faithfully built the beautiful, healthy Church we have today. Your prayers and continued embrace of our values of relationship help others overcome their own 42 moments. I truly am honored and proud to serve you as Pastor. And thanks for letting me tell my story over and over again.

To Margie Hernandez. When you and Eddie came to Metro, it seemed like you were stepping into a new season of life as you stepped away from the church you had known your whole life. Little did I know you were sent to Metro for Mary and I. When I needed a cardiologist you introduced me to your boss, Dr. Rajesh Dhairyawan. For the last 15 years, you've monitored my health, kept me a priority in office visits, and given Mary and me peace of mind.

To our pastors, Mike and Kathy Hayes. Mary, myself, and our Metro Life Church are forever grateful for the way you came in and righted the ship when it seemed all hell was coming against us. You immediately dropped everything that you were doing to come be with us as Mary and I recouped. You stepped into the pulpit that next Sunday and let the Church know we would all overcome. You then met with our staff and calmed their fears and steadied their faith. Honor isn't something I give because of what you are doing today but because of what you did in the past. So I continue to honor you and I'm blessed to call you my Pastors.

To paramedics Cliff Williams, Jim Mooney, Rich Hunter, Thomas Conti, and Randy Spiegelhalter, thank you for saving my life and keeping me around to be a husband, father, and pastor. I can't imagine missing out on this life. The one I've been privileged to live thanks to your hard work and life-saving dedication. When you visited me in the hospital and mentioned you worked on me for forty-two minutes before transport to the hospital, you gave life to what would become my mantra of helping others through their own 42 moments. Today, I have an even greater respect for the First Responders who selflessly serve our society. Pretty interesting how that night was the first and only time all of you had worked together. Evidently there was a much higher purpose the Creator had planned. My prayer is that you would know the power of the One who inspired you to give me one last shot of the new medication for my resuscitation. It was Rich who said in a text, "The minute we pushed that med through the IV and shocked you one more time, it fixed you, and you stabilized." I'm forever grateful you gave it one more shot...one more try before giving up.

And lastly, a big thanks to Jordan Loftis from Story Chorus for helping me put this experience into words. I couldn't get this story out for the last fifteen years as the memory of it all was just so emotional; not because of the pain, but because of the reality of knowing the outcome was so close to being different. Now, through this book, we can help others stay in the ring, keep fighting until they finish strong, and leave a legacy of blessing.

About the Author

Lead Pastor Steve Alessi founded Metro Life Church in Doral, Florida, in 1997 with his wife, Mary, and serves as a spiritual guide to all who walk through its doors. He was called into the ministry at the age of nineteen and has fulfilled this calling in good faith for more than thirty years.

After graduating from Southeastern University in 1984, Steve served alongside his parents as an Associate Pastor for thirteen years before establishing Metro Life. When his parents, John and Ann, retired in 2013, Steve and Mary accepted the responsibilities as the Lead Pastors of Grace Church as well. Together, they transformed it into the Dadeland Campus of Metro Life Church, uniting the two congregations as one Church family.

Through his ministry, Steve strives to make a positive impact on the lives of congregants and members of the community at large. He is proud of the church's growing local campus and its vibrant, innovative online offerings. One of his newest initiatives is the Goodfellas Camp, a retreat where men who are committed to God can connect, unwind, and deepen their understanding of faith and Man Up.

Steve contributes to the local community as a member of the Miami-Dade County Interfaith Advisory Board (IAB) and as a Chaplain for the Doral Police Department. He is also a member of the Champions Network with Pastor Joel Osteen.

Steve feels blessed to have his family by his side and enjoys the help and support of his son and daughter-in-law, Christopher and Richelle, and his three daughters, Lauren, Gabrielle, and Stephanie, along with Stephanie's husband, Chris Muina. Steve is also delighted to take on the title of Papa to Chris and Stephanie's daughter, Gianna, and Christopher and Richelle's newest addition to the Alessi legacy arriving May 2023, Marino John Alessi. In fact, the family regularly opens up about the joys and challenges of working together in their weekly podcast, *The Family Business with The Alessi's*. In his spare time, Steve enjoys time in the woods at his farm in Georgia and hunting with his family and friends.

Connect with Steve at MetroLifeChurch.com and AlessiFamilyBusiness.com.